Jazz & Improvised Piano

James Taylor

A **new** approach, enabling any pianist possessing basic technical skills to improvise.

YouCaxton Publications

24 High Street, Bishop's Castle, Shropshire. SY3 8JX
www.youCaxton.co.uk

Published in Great Britain by
James Taylor

Copyright © James Taylor 2013

The Author asserts the moral right to
be identified as the author of this work.

ISBN 978-1-909644-03-8

Printed and bound in Great Britain.

All rights reserved. No part of this publication may be reproduced, stored in a retrieval system, or transmitted in any form or by any means, electronic, mechanical, photocopying, recording or otherwise, without the prior permission of the publisher.

This book is sold subject to the condition that it shall not, by way of trade or otherwise, be lent, re-sold, hired out or otherwise circulated without the publisher's prior consent in any form of binding or cover other than that in which it is published and without a similar condition including this condition being imposed on the subsequent purchaser.

Dedication

This course is dedicated to all my students at Shrewsbury School as a thank you for their valuable input; the course evolved through teaching these students over a period of about ten years. Also, I would like to extend my thanks to John Moore, who gave me the opportunity to work there, and to Karen Wilding, for her endless help and patience as she printed out numerous early versions – and indeed there were many!

Further thanks are extended to Chris Shelley and Bob Jeffrey for pointing out various unclear explanations - this was immensely helpful for me in my quest for clarity. I hope that you will find my instructions easy to follow - every effort has been made to break things down into manageable chunks. The aim is to take your knowledge from nought to highly competent in a single volume, so the course may take up to a year to complete. This can be, and has been done. Enjoy.

JT

There is no conventional music notation in this book. The purpose of the book is to explain the processes involved in finding the chords, and notation would have bypassed the chord-finding processes which, once learned, can be applied to any key. The route is tougher, but far more rewarding in terms of helping you navigate the keyboard - this ability to navigate being central to the skill of improvisation. If you are a classical pianist at any level who wants to play music without needing written down music notation, this book will liberate you.

I intend to produce a DVD to accompany this book soon, this DVD being effectively a set of lessons in which I will talk you through each lesson, giving you step-by-step visual illustrations of the procedures and live demonstrations of the improvisations. Meanwhile, the most useful parts of the book are those discussing ways of finding chords, and these are very carefully put together, guiding you step-by-step along the way. Some of the improvisations might be hard to grasp without the extra guidance of the DVD, but you will still be able to retrieve the basic concepts and make music from the descriptions.

Contents

Introduction _____ 1

The approach (in a nutshell) _____ 1

Comparing a 'Classical pianist' to a 'Jazz pianist' _____ 1

The elements of piano improvisation _____ 3

Lesson one: some notes to play with _____ 5

Lesson two: some more notes to play with _____ 6

Lesson three: exploring the use of pedal _____ 7

Swing feel _____ 8

Lesson four: introducing the blues scale _____ 10

Lesson five: more improvisations _____ 12

Lesson six: fun with triads _____ 12

Film music improvisation _____ 13

Lesson seven: shells _____ 17

Lesson eight: Blue Monk, our first jazz piece _____ 18

Lesson nine: let's start some harmony _____ 18

The minor 7 chord _____ 19

Finding a minor 9th chord _____ 19

Lesson ten: major 7th chords _____ 21

Lesson eleven: the 2 – 5 – 1 in a major key _____ 23

Lesson twelve: play Misty for me _____ 28

More about the 7th chord _____ 29

Lesson thirteen: more about modes _____ 31

Lesson fourteen: Pentatonic scales, improvisation in modes, and playing outside modes __ 33

Funk and modern improvisations to play _____ 34

How to find a 'so what' chord _____ 35

A little more about playing outside the mode _____ 36

Another way to find notes outside the dorian mode _____ 37

Lesson fifteen: the minor 2 – 5 – 1	37
Finding a 7th chord with sharpened 5th and sharpened 9th (Altered chord)	38
A cheat method to find the altered chord	39
Lesson sixteen: Introducing the walking bass and the tritone substitution	41
Solo version of Autumn Leaves using shells	43
Lesson seventeen: 11th chords	44
More about left hand voicings	45
Another voicing for the 2 – 5 – 1 in a major key	45
Another voicing for the 2 – 5 – 1 in a minor key	46
Concluding remarks	47
Additional help for more advanced players. Easy ways to find difficult modes	47
The super locrian mode.	48
The locrian sharp 2 mode	48
The Lydian dominant mode	49
The Lydian augmented mode	50
The whole tone scale	50
The diminished scale	51
The 5th mode of the harmonic minor scale	52
Additional jazz voicings, available when a bass player is present	52
Additional substitutions similar to the tritone substitution	55
Putting it all together	56
About ear training	57
A little bit more	59

Introduction

I have seen many talented musicians develop from children into teenagers, gradually becoming young people with a love of playing music. Many of these students went on to play in bands, some of these bands enjoying commercial success, but most importantly, all of these students can enjoy being able to just sit down and improvise something at the piano. This book will lift the curtain of mystique surrounding improvisation, destroying the myth that you can either do it or you can't, and it will show you exactly what is happening when an improviser is in the process of improvisation. You will learn that, far from plucking ideas out of thin air, the process of improvisation involves building on known structures, and following numerous rules and concepts in order to produce a pleasing result. One caveat; this book is written for people of teenage years and upwards, and for adults who wish to explore improvised music; the hand-spans required to cover the notes make it unsuitable for young children. Hopefully I will be asked to write another book for children, and another for people looking for still more advanced jazz knowledge. I sincerely hope that my experience as a teacher has enabled me to produce a course that is reasonably easy to follow. The learning curve is steep, and there is a lot to learn, but I have aimed to get you there via the easiest and most direct route.

JT

The approach (in a nutshell)

I generally find that I have two groups of students: those who can improvise but who know little theory, and those who know a lot of theory but cannot improvise. Ironically, those who can improvise will usually pick up the theory quite quickly, whereas those who know a lot of theory tend to continue amassing more knowledge but struggle to progress. This course is running with this observation and with my own personal experience as a teacher of jazz piano; for this reason it differs from any other approach. You will first be offered a number of improvisations with very little structure, and this will force you to become highly creative. You'll have to make up your own chords out of vague guidelines, and you'll have to make up rhythms and melodic fragments, and through joining all your ideas together you will learn how to improvise. This will give you the skill that you can then use to accumulate your knowledge of theory through learning how theory is actually applied, i.e., through improvisation itself. When we look at jazz theory we will find alternative and easier ways to find complex jazz chords, and similarly, when we look at jazz scales (modes) we will be using easier methods to find them. There are also a number of 'ways of thinking' that can hold back our progress, so I'll discuss these in the following paragraphs.

Comparing a 'Classical pianist' to a 'Jazz pianist'

Many musicians are actually afraid to experiment with improvisation! Understanding why so many classical musicians feel they are unable to play jazz will help to clarify exactly what thought processes are involved in the task of playing jazz, and this knowledge will help us to avoid imposing certain restrictions on our own musical creations. These are restrictions that we automatically impose, outside of our awareness, which may slow down our progress. When we improvise at the piano, in order to be most creative we need to be completely uninhibited, and we need to feel free to produce any sound without judgment. We need to evaluate rather than judge. We must feel free to listen to and evaluate each sound as we hear it, evaluating how we could use the note in our construction. It might be a nice sound or a nasty sound, but each sound has to be listened to and investigated for its own merits, since every sound will carry a set of harmonic and melodic implications. The most important thing is to learn the properties of every available combination of notes, because every sound has a place of its own in a fitting context. When we know these sounds, we can build up tension by steering into the nasty sounds, and then we can resolve these 'dissonant' sounds into more pleasant sounds. Through learning the properties of all of the sounds available to us we can learn how to string them together.

A classical player may be distressed when they play something dissonant, and may even stop playing! Ironically, when a dissonant sound is struck, it is most useful to continue playing, since this provides an opportunity to learn how to resolve dissonance. The resolution of dissonance (nasty sounds) to consonance (nice sounds) is one of the driving forces of music, and it is just as important that we explore the dissonant sounds as it is that we explore the consonant sounds. We notice how a classical musician will want to produce instant music of the same quality as Mozart and will fear hitting a wrong note, i.e., an unintentional note, and these wants can seriously impede progress in playing jazz. These inhibitions are completely natural, because they are inbuilt through practising classical music, where a musician will strive towards a perfect performance of a set piece of music – in this context, an unintentional note is obviously a wrong note. Once these self-inflicted restrictions are recognised and dealt with, a classical player is free to become a highly competent jazz player. Highlighting the differences between playing classical music and playing improvised music is possibly the most important issue raised in this book, since this clarifies the issues that prevent many talented players from getting off the starting blocks. In fact, the same self-restrictive issues affect many non-classical musicians who dabble in jazz but fail to realise their full potential.

Tip: If you ever recoil after hitting an unintentional note, play it again and ask yourself 'how can I make this note sound good?'. Any note can be used to good effect if you can use it in the right way, so aim to work out a context where it would sound good.

With the risk of repeating myself, when a classical musician first experiments with improvisation, ESPECIALLY a highly trained musician with a good sense of pitch, there is a feeling of inadequacy. They want to generate instant music at the level of a great musician (which isn't going to happen), and the result is frustration. Ironically, these people are much more capable of finding the notes of their choice than a less able classical musician, so why do they find that their music 'isn't working' as well as that of a less competent classical musician playing jazz? The answer to this question is central to the way we think when we play jazz. It is the core to unleashing any person's ability to improvise.

A classical pianist has every note set out for him, and to a large extent the way he plays those notes is also set out. A jazz pianist on the other hand might have nothing more than a few symbols written down, which tell the pianist the general structure of the music. We could compare classical music to assembling a bookshelf from a flat pack, and we could compare jazz improvisation to being handed some pencils and asked to draw something non-specific, e.g., a dog. When assembling the bookshelf, everything has to be in the correct place, whereas when drawing the picture, YOU get to choose the type of dog, the colour of the dog etc.

We can all improvise. As children, we improvise language before we speak. Quite possibly, as you grew into a toddler you would have improvised conversations with imaginary friends. Despite this, if I asked you to stand up right now and talk about anything, absolutely anything, you would probably stall and ask "...but what should I talk about?". Although you had been offered complete freedom, your worries about looking silly would be freezing your creativity. On the other hand, if I said "Tell me what you had for breakfast, and tell me how your morning went", you would probably talk for some time, going into great detail about the toast getting burned and the smoke alarms going off. Lack of instruction can cause our minds to 'freeze up', even though the reality is that we have complete freedom to do anything. However, with a little work you can learn to embrace this freedom, and embracing this same freedom will enable us to improvise.

When I began teaching jazz, I had a couple of students who were also drummers. To my astonishment, these were among my best students. I never had anything preconceptions about drummer's musical abilities, but let's just say that this was unexpected. What was going on?

An improvisation DOESN'T NEED a lot of notes, or even a sequence of carefully chosen notes. What it does need is a STRUCTURE. Rhythm is at the very heart of musical structure, and an improvisation can sound satisfactory even if you only use two notes, providing the rhythmic structure is good. Try this out for yourself. Drum a rhythm on a table with two fingers, then go to the piano and choose any two notes (one for each finger) and drum a rhythm on these two notes. Notice how complete this two-note tune can sound, and how it can stand alone as a musical entity.

When improvising jazz, it is of enormous help to have some sort of backing drum beat for support. This provides a framework from which the student can hang ideas, (particularly rhythmic ideas!); for example, they might play accented chords either on the beats or on the off-beats. As a teacher, when a student is improvising, I tend to tap any nearby surface, providing an appropriate 'backing rhythm' for the student. Tapping on a pocket holding coins is curiously effective!

Bearing this in mind, it is important that the student understands that an improvisation can work even if we choose a fairly random set of notes, providing the rhythm is good. I say this because so many students search so hard for good notes and lines, and this stops the flow of rhythmic ideas, which in turn stops their improvisation from 'working'.

The elements of improvisation

There are two important elements needed in order to become a competent improviser. The first is an ability to improvise, i.e. to develop rhythms and melodic shapes at the piano and to link them together, the second ingredient is a thorough knowledge of the theory behind the sounds that we produce, this knowledge giving us an abundance of harmonic resources, such as modes (jazz scales), chords, substitutions, and a wealth of theories, many of which I will explain later.

Jazz music, like music in general, tends to consist of three ingredients working together. A bass player will nail down the harmony, a piano or guitar will provide chords, and a singer, saxophone player, or trumpet player will play the tune or improvisation on top. As pianists, we can play any one, or any combination of these roles, at any one moment. The roles we play are often dictated by the set-up in which we find ourselves playing. For example:

1. If we are playing as a duo with someone who plays a melody line, such as a saxophone player or a singer, we will play a bass line (left hand) and some chords (right hand). This will give a supporting texture over which the other player can improvise or play the melody.

2. If we have a bass player with us, they will play the bass line while we play both chords (left hand,) and melody/improvisation (right hand).

3. If we are in a band with a bass player and a melody line player, we can play very full chords using both hands. This gives us lots of scope for finding interesting extended chords.

4. If we are playing alone, we have to provide all three, or switch between the three enough to make the music 'work'. This is tough, and takes a lot of practise, but the most helpful advice you will ever get is to use rhythm as imaginatively as you can.

We can find ourselves playing in any of these contexts, and the situation will often change when we solo (= take our turn to improvise) because some of the other players will stop playing to give us more space (musically speaking). In a duo context, we will be playing alone when we solo, and so we will have to play as if we were in a solo context for the duration of our improvisation.

This need to fulfil a number of roles means that a pianist has a much more challenging job than other players; a saxophonist only has to play a top line, a bass player only has to play a bottom line, but as pianists, we have to learn the mechanics of both, together with accumulating as complete a knowledge of chords as we can grasp. Because of this, we will have to study walking bass lines and extended chords, in addition to the modes that our single-line friends are studying. As you progress through the book, always bear this in mind. Some of the pieces I have set will sound great as solo piano performances, but others will provide practise in playing various combinations of roles.

Although I am writing this book as a series of lessons, the intention is for the student to keep playing the material from the earlier sections, adding more material to it as they go along. Improvisation is a process of growth, and every time you improvise over the same material you will find new things you can do. Every time you play, go over the improvisations you have already learned, looking for new approaches and new melodic/rhythmic ideas.

We will be systematically looking at sets of notes, calling them modes or scales, and these will provide a resource of notes we can select from for our improvisations; when practising these, you will accidentally play some notes that are outside the mode/ scale. When this happens, listen to the notes and assess how you might use them in an improvisation. Think about how you could include them, because it will certainly be possible to use them effectively if you can build a suitable melodic context. For the time being, assume that there is no such thing as a wrong note – think of these notes as 'notes that we haven't learned how to use yet'. Having said this, it is a good idea to stick to the scales we are practising so that we can learn the qualities of each particular scale, learning the sounds attached to each particular combination of notes. We will be expanding these scales and learning how one scale can lead into another, and how each scale has its own unique sound. If we deliberately chose not to stick to the scales we set out to practice, we would never learn the licks and riffs available within the context of each scale, in fact we would fail to learn any structure at all. Explore freely, but always look for some sort of musical structure. You can break the rules any time you like, as long as you know what you are doing. So, we have to strive to learn all the theory, all the relevant scales, and all the relevant harmony, and from this position of knowledge we can deliberately play notes that are outside our scales to great effect. Play the pieces that follow, which allow you to compose freely, thus allowing your playing to develop through your musical exploration. You will have a lot of freedom in the first few pieces, in some of these you will be free to select any black notes you choose. Gradually you will be introduced to the essential theory that you will need in order to play any jazz piece you wish.

Some notes to play with

These first improvisations enable the student to play as freely as they choose, as they select notes from a given scale. In these particular pieces, any note chosen from the scale shown will sound good, so there is no fear of playing wrong notes. The purpose is to give the student something to play without the restrictions of a chord sequence, and provided they stick to the choice of notes given, they can explore and build a musical entity which can be as long and as dramatic as they choose. This will build up the skills of improvisation.

Lesson One

Here the student plays on the black notes, adding the occasional 'B'. The feel of this improvisation is essentially rock. The student plays an octave G flat in the left hand while the right hand improvises on any chosen black notes. The left hand can move to a 'B', and can also choose to move to other notes in octaves. For example, try E flats, then D flats, then Bs, these other notes adding to the variety.

To get you started, the right hand could play a triad of G flat major in second inversion, voiced D flat G flat B flat going from bottom to top (left hand plays a G flat octave). After this chord you could play an A flat then a G flat then play the chord again. Left hand can start with two low G flats an octave apart (called an octave G flat), then can move to an octave B. When the left hand plays an octave B, your right hand might replace the D flat in the chord with an E flat (optional). The left hand could then move to E flats, then to D flats, then to a B again, and then freely move around this selection of notes.

The right hand can be working around the pattern suggested, as you generate a rock rhythm between the hands. You can also include Bs in the right hand, particularly in falling patterns B – B flat – A flat – G flat.

You can use the pedal continuously, but notice that the lower notes become a bit mixed up if you hold it down all the time. Experiment releasing the pedal to get rid of unwanted notes, then press the pedal back down and enjoy the fullness of the sound. We will examine the use of the pedal shortly.

Use this exercise to generate a musical texture and to develop good rhythm between the hands, adding extra notes (generally black notes) as you discover the extra sounds that are available.

Lesson Two:
Some more notes to play with

The second piece has a sort of 'Indian' feel to it, due to the oriental mode it is based on (5th mode of F harmonic minor).This, together with the underpinning rhythm (even quavers-crotchet=120), lends it available for many improvisational effects and much experimentation. You can hold the (right) pedal down throughout your improvisation because all the notes are compatible with each other. Aim to use rhythm as a means of creating excitement as much as possible. When I teach this piece, I close the piano lid and ask my students to drum on the wood of the lid before they play. The student can practice drumming equal quavers with random accents on the piano lid, and, having established a basic feel for the piece, can extend their ideas, making up their own rhythms. When I teach, I can join in with supporting and/or interacting rhythms, and we can work together to create exciting drumming rhythms together. After this work, the student will have a wealth of rhythmic ideas which they can transfer to their improvisation as they improvise at the piano, stringing notes together using these rhythms. Remember that you don't have to use lots of different notes. In fact, you can stay on one note and play various rhythms on it if you choose.

The left hand can support the improvisation by playing two Cs an octave apart, which can either be played together, or one C might be held while the other is re-iterated like a drum beat. Even quavers with random accents throughout.

The right hand selects notes from the mode **E, F, G, B flat, C**, selecting three or four notes at a time and building small rhythmic units out of these; units of three notes can be repeated, e.g. E, F,G, E, F,G, F, G, B flat ,F, G, B flat etc., moving the pattern freely over the whole range of keyboard but restricting ourselves to the notes of the mode. This can be made more exciting by including groups of two notes, e.g. E, F, G, E, F, G, E, F, E, F, G, E, F, G, E, F etc.

In addition to the linear improvisation, we can create chords out of the mode. Just select any cluster of notes from the mode and play them all together.

The right hand can also include notes outside the mode, which can be made into features. Explore the sounds generated by including a **D flat**, then return to using exclusively notes from the mode, then explore the sounds you can generate by including an **A flat.**

Although the left hand is basically holding down the C at the bottom, it can also move up and play some chords (consisting of notes from the mode). This offers more exciting rhythmic support for the right hand.

Lesson Three:
Exploring the use of pedal

Play a note at the bottom of the piano. Hold it down and count how many seconds it lasts for. Now play a note at the top of the piano. You will find that a low note will last a lot longer than a high notes. Because of this, we can hold low notes on with the pedal and then take both hands to the higher register of the piano, the lower notes will continue sounding while the higher notes sound and fade. We can make up patterns using both hands and explore some piano 'effects'. Applying this to the piece in lesson two, play the low 'C' octave as in the first lesson, then while keeping the pedal down, move both hands to the higher notes on the piano and use both hands to generate effects using notes exclusively from our E, F, G, B flat, C, mode.

The pedal is used to hold down notes that we want to keep sounding, while we play other additional notes on top. If all the notes we play belong to the same chord, the effect is good. A problem arises if the chords change and we hold the pedal down, because then we hear two chords at the same time and the result is a confused sound. To get around this, we have to filter out the old harmony while holding on to the new. We can practise this 'filtering' with this following exercise.

1. Using one finger, play any low note on the piano, then press the sustain pedal (right pedal).

2. Keep the pedal down and take your finger off the piano key. The note should continue sounding, because the pedal is holding it.

3. While keeping the pedal down, play another low note. You should now hear two low notes, the old note and the new note.

4. Keeping the new note held down with your finger, lift the pedal up until (only) the old note stops sounding, then press the pedal back down. You should still have your finger holding the new note.

5. You can now take your finger off this note and it will continue sounding, since the pedal is holding it for you. This is equivalent to the situation in step 2.

6. Move from note to note in the same way in order to practise your pedal technique. The exercise is most effective if your hand leaves the keyboard completely between notes, since this ensures that your pedal is right down and that (only) the pedal is holding the note for you.

Notice that if neither pedal or finger are down we have no sound, so one or the other – or both - will be down at any given time within this exercise. Pedal technique takes practice, so it will probably take a few sessions of diligent work before you get the hang of this.

Swing feel

Read and work on this section first, before you move on to practice the exercises which look at the blues scale. You will be using the rhythm work in this section to enable your jazz playing to swing. To play a blues swing solo we need to be able to play a swing rhythm, so we'll turn our attention to rhythm to lay this crucial foundation.

As we discussed in the introduction, rhythm is the most essential structural dimension we can use to generate a satisfactory solo. Swing feel is a bit like a set of dotted notes in 4/4 time, only it has a 'compound time' feel to it. It is, in fact, very nearly a classical 12/8 time (12/8 is 4 equal groups each of 3 quavers). If this were written in 12/8 it would be crotchet quaver, crotchet quaver, crotchet quaver, crotchet quaver. However, there are important differences as to how a classical player would play this and how a jazz musician would play a solo which 'swings'. If you play classical music, once you know how the two differ, you will be able to play both.

1. A classical musician will play a bar of 4/4 with the strongest beats being 1 and 3, the first beat being the stronger of the two. On the other hand, a Jazz musician will stress beats 2 and 4.

2. A classical musician will accent the notes that are on the beats more than the notes that are off the beat, whereas a jazz musician will accent notes which are off the beat, i.e. between the main beats, more frequently than the notes on the beat. In our 12/8 bar of crotchet quaver, crotchet quaver, crotchet quaver, crotchet quaver, the quavers are the off-beat notes.

The following tapping/clapping exercises will assist in getting your own, or your student's playing, to 'swing'.

Swing rhythm exercise

1. Make sure that beats 2 and 4 are the stronger beats than 1 and 3. To achieve this, start by counting out loud, 4 even beats to the bar (|one..two..three..four..|one..two..three..four|), and while counting, clap/tap on 2 and 4, being sure to stress these beats – |one..**two**..three..**four**..|one..**two**..three..**four**|.

    You could also practice this by counting one, two, three, four, one two three four etc, accenting beats two and four by speaking them louder than one and three.

2. Clap a bar of swinging quavers in 4/4 accenting the off-beats. Again, think of this as a 12/8 time with alternate crotchets and quavers as before. Accent the quavers.

    |1 **&**2 **&**3 **&**4 **&**|1 **&**2 **&**3 **&**4 **&**|

    This exercise could be spoken, counting bars of four beats, and stressing the 'ands' in between the main beats: one, **and** two, **and** three, **and** four, **and**.

    This is a lot more challenging than it sounds, and will probably take a considerable amount of practice. Make the main beats, i.e. the one, two, three and four, as quiet as possible – only the 'ands' are loud!

After mastering this, leave out the main beats, only playing the off-beats. Precede this with a straight bar of 4 crotchets like this:

|1..2..3..4 &|rest &rest &rest &rest|1..2..3..4 &|rest &rest &rest &rest|

Now make up a few swing rhythms out of similar building blocks, and extend them for 20 bars or thereabouts. Have some fun making up lots of jazzy rhythms. This sort of practise is some of the most rewarding practice you can do because it teaches you where you can put the notes. Knowing which notes you can put in these places is almost secondary when it comes to producing a jazz improvisation.

Many jazz pianists know all the relevant scales, but are very frustrated because they cannot produce a jazz solo that works. They may spend hours looking for new licks, but even after learning these, they cannot make their improvisation 'work'/'swing'. The frustration is compounded when they hear another local pianist play something very basic which 'works' extremely well. The difference is the same as that between the classical player who improvises and the sweaty drummer who improvises, and is solely down to rhythm. Diligent practice of the exercises I have presented will prevent this embarrassment happening to you!

Having practised these rhythm exercises, remember that when you play a solo (improvise) at this stage, the order of notes is not important. Think of improvising as being like playing a set of drums, the piano keys being the drums.

Many classical players find it hard to keep a regular pulse when they play jazz - this is a problem that is caused through trying too hard to keep the time steady. What happens is that the mind tries to consciously gauge the length of each pulse, shutting down our body rhythm, and so our rhythmic resources divert to a less reliable timekeeping device. We have an inbuilt body clock which we use when we sway in time to music we like to listen to, or when we dance, and this is a completely automatic natural response. If we think too hard about our time-keeping, we cause tension, which can cause this natural body response to shut down, leaving us reliant on our mental ability to guess time. This leaves us struggling to keep in time, and also makes it very hard to produce a swinging improvisation. You will tense up if you try to consciously gauge time, so always relax and let your body respond naturally in order to make your jazz improvisation swing and flow. Feel the rhythm, and let it flow from your body.

Lesson Four:
Introducing the blues scale

We've seen now how we can use certain modes, and how provided that we stick to the notes within these modes, we can play any note, or any string of notes we choose. Also, we have enjoyed the freedom to experiment with rhythmic ideas and build musical 'structures'. Now we're going to look at another mode - the blues scale. When we move from any note on the piano up to the closest note left or right (whether black or white) we are said to be moving up a semitone. We can use these semitones to help us to find the blues scale starting from any note. Counting up the piano in semitones from the starting note (step=semitone), we have 3 steps between the first two notes, 2 steps between the next two, one step between the next two, then up another step, then 3 steps, then 2 steps (reaching an octave above the starting note), giving us a framework of 321132, which we can use to find our blues scale in any key; for example in the key of C:

C ..3steps ..Eflat ..2steps.. F ..1step.. Fsharp.. 1step.. G ..3steps.. Bflat ..2steps ..C

This system can be transferred freely to any key of our choice; you can simply choose the starting note, then count up 3 steps for the next note, then up 2 steps, then 1 then 1 then 3 then 2, and you will have found the notes belonging to the wanted blues scale.

Exercise:

Find the blues scale starting on 'C'. Now find the blues scale starting on G, now find the blues scale starting on F. Now find the blues scale starting on A.

Now find the blues scale starting on 'E flat'. What do you notice? Yes, all the notes apart from 'A' are black. This is useful for our improvisation practice, since we can play freely on the black notes with no fear of playing outside the scale.

Right hand alone, and using exclusively the notes of 'C' blues scale, improvise a medium swing solo - use the region of the keyboard just below middle 'C'. Make it really 'bluesy'. Now do the same for 'E flat' blues. Before doing this, it is a good idea to go over the section on swing rhythm again.

Really think about your use of rhythm. Go over the rhythm exercises in the previous section (Swing feel) and apply the rhythmic devices you have learned as much as you can. Here is a little exercise to help you:

Exercise:

Apply the rhythm |1 &2 &3 &4 | (accenting the &'s)to the notes C – **E flat** – F – **G flat** – F – **E flat** C, making the E flats and the G flats a lot louder than the Cs and Fs (They're in bold to help you apply this). Similarly, apply the rhythm|1 &2 &3 &4|to a descending blues scale, i.e. C – **Bflat** - G – **Gflat** - F - **Eflat** – C, and then apply 1 &2 to rising G – **Bflat** – C. In addition to playing the notes in bold louder, aim to play the other notes as quietly as possible. This makes everything instantly sound a lot better, and will be enough to make any blues solo 'work'. Also be sure to join your notes and play legato.

Play the same ideas in other blues scales, i.e., play the same riffs starting on different notes, remembering the strong accents on the &s.

A number of Jazz pieces use a descending bass line(C-B flat-A flat-G in even minims). We can borrow this and use it to develop ideas for improvising on the blues scale. Play this bass figure in the left hand, while your right hand can improvise, playing a C blues-scale based improvisation in swing rhythm. Make up a couple of very simple riffs, maybe only two or three notes long, and use these with lots of repetition in your improvisation to give you a starting point. Let the left hand lead, and when you begin, play very little in the right hand, keeping your focus on the left hand, which keeps a constant pulse throughout.

Notice that the left hand figure, descending **C, B flat, A flat, G**, follows a descending pattern. It goes down 2steps, then 2 steps, then 1 step. We can use this pattern, and starting from the note of our choice, we can count down in semitones, **2,2,1**, and this will enable us to find this bass line in any key. For example, starting from a low F, the next note would be 2 steps lower (E flat), then the next note 2 steps below that (D flat), then the final note would be 1 step below that (C).

Since we can already find the blues scale in any key, we can transpose and use this bass figure to provide some bass for our chosen key, enabling us to practise improvising in any chosen blues scale. Find F blues again, and improvise in this, while your left hand supports it by playing the descending bass figure starting on F. Now do the same for G blues, and then E flat blues.

It is worthwhile practising the blues scale in a number of keys, since this will greatly accelerate your gaining mastery of the keyboard. The blues scales also sound slightly different in different keys, so this practice will keep your mind fresh and help to inspire you to create more ideas.

Another way to find the blues scale is this:

- Find the minor triad in the key you want. For C this would be C, Elat, and G. In technical terms these are the root, third, and fifth.

- We keep all the notes of this triad because they are all members of the blues scale. We keep the fifth, but we add the note a step below it, and also we add the note a step below that. So in C we would add G flat and F.

So far, working in C we have C, Eflat, F, Gflat, and G.

- We find the root an octave above the start note of the scale, which is of course in the scale, then we add the note 2 steps below it. So working in C we would find the upper C then we would come down 2 steps and find Bflat.

Now we have the complete blues scale. Working from the bottom up in C we have C, Eflat, F, Gflat, G, Bflat, and C.

This is useful because when improvising we can find the blues scale as (while) we improvise. We can first improvise using only the notes in the minor triad, then from here we can easily add the two notes below the fifth and we can start including these, then finally we can find the top two notes and start including these.

This method is better than the 321132 method in that it is faster and easier, it can be used WHILE you play, and also it is clearer how the notes relate to the start note. It's also better for seeing how the blues scale can be made out of a minor 7 chord. It's a last minute insertion to irritate my book production team.

Lesson Five:
More improvisations

We can play a 'Spanish' sounding improvisation. The left hand can play an octave 'E' and the right hand plays major triads on E, F and G. Aim to generate a rhythm between the hands to sound something like a flamenco guitar.

After this, your left hand can play the chords while your right hand plays on the white notes with an added G sharp. (This is E Phrygian with an added G sharp). Alternate left hand octave/right hand chords with left hand chords/right hand improvised solo. The right hand might include repeating (ostinato) figures, particularly triplet figures, on the white notes.

Lesson Six:
Fun with triads

If we exclusively play white notes, we can have fun using a number of triads. We've got C major,(C, E, G bottom to top) as a starting point, from here we could experiment going to A minor (A, C, E), G major (G, B, D), F major, E minor or D minor. Start with a C major triad and experiment - your right hand playing the triads while your left hand plays the roots of the chords (e.g . RH plays C triad while LH plays a low C, then perhaps RH plays G triad while LH plays G).

A more exciting version - rather than the left hand playing the roots of each chord, the left hand can stay on one note while the right hand plays different triads over the top. For example, the left hand might play (and re-iterate) a low octave C while the right hand plays triads of C major, F major, G major, D minor etc. After this, the left hand might move to play and hold a low octave F while the right hand plays triads of F major, G major, A minor, D minor etc. When you do this, it is possible to improvise on white notes between the chords.

When the left hand plays the long, low octave Cs and Fs, you might like to hold the bottom note of each octave and re-iterate the top one or vice versa.

If you know how to find inversions of triads, you can include these. An inversion is where the notes of the triad are rearranged; for example, C major triad, C, E, G, (bottom to top) can be rearranged to E, G, C, or G, C, E.

Also, from any triad you might experiment moving some elements while others stay in place. For example, from C major triad, C, E, G, you might keep only the G in place and move the other elements - you might move to B, D, G, then to A, C, G, and then back to B, D, G. Similarly, keeping only the C in place, C, E, G, might move to C, F, A, then to C, G, B, and then back to C, F, A.

The right hand can improvise in 6ths quite freely. (a 6th is when two notes, 6 notes apart, are played simultaneously. For example, E and C, or D and B, or F and D. I've written the lower note first in each of these pairs.

You can also play the triads with your left hand, while your right hand improvises freely on the white notes. When you do this you can arpeggiate the left hand triads, i.e., rather than playing all the notes together, play them one after another.

Film music improvisation

This is based on triads and is an extremely useful exercise. It sounds great, and it offers fantastic scope for harmonic exploration: the left land exploring triads, the right hand exploring modes.

Labelling the notes of the scale

Starting on C, work up the white notes of the piano. Notice we are playing a major scale. We can think of the first note as note one (C in this case), the second note as note two (D in this case), the third note as note three (E) and so on.

The left hand part for Film Music improvisation.

1. The major triad of C consists of three notes; C, E, and G (working from bottom to top). These are notes one, three, and five in C major. We can juggle these notes, putting the E up an octave. This will give us C, G, and E, working from the bottom upwards.

2. We can add a D (note 2 in C major scale, referred to either as a 2nd or a 0th) to this combination, and we can play a flowing left hand accompaniment figure **C G D E** in quavers (from the bottom up). Hold the top note (E) to complete a bar of 4/4 time.

3. Because we are working in C major scale, the right hand can improvise freely on white notes. We might include a few 6ths here, they will sound great. For example, the right hand might play a G and an E (G at the bottom) and move to an E and a C, moving freely either in steps, or larger intervals.

    Notice that your right hand can play any white note, but you might still feel as if you are using some wrong notes. Again, this is not because the note is wrong, it is because you haven't yet discovered how to put it in a context where it sounds good. When you feel that a note is wrong, for example the note F, see if you can find a way to use it effectively. Clue, the note F will want to resolve downwards onto an E, and this sounds good because we have a dissonance resolving to a consonance, tension resolving to relaxation, the driving force in music. Once again, evaluate the notes you hear, never judge right or wrong or you will slow down your progress considerably.

Now, back to our scale of C for a little more theory. Working up the scale of C, and using only notes in the scale (white notes) we can build some triads. C major triad is based on the first note of C major scale, so we'll call it **chord one**. Similarly, building a triad based on the second note D, gives us a D minor triad (D, F, and A), so we'll call this **chord two**. With this knowledge, move on to the next part of our film music improvisation.

We are using the notes of C major scale, and we can continue working using only these white notes, only our left hand will move to **chord four**, the chord of F major.

4. Chord of F: The left hand can now play the same flowing accompaniment figure, but this time it will start on F, using the notes **F, C, G, and A**, - in ascending order - while the right hand continues to improvise freely on the white notes.

5. We can play a few bars in F before moving back to our C major accompaniment figure. We can freely play a few bars in F before moving to C, or vice versa. This sounds good, and you might choose to stick to these two chords, moving between C and F, until you feel ready to move on.

The chords of C and F are chords one and four in the key of C, we can now introduce chord 6 (A minor) and chord two (D minor).

6. For chord six, A minor, the left hand can play the same type of flowing accompaniment figure, giving us **A,E,B,C.** This will happily follow either chord one (C - left hand C,G,D,E) or chord four (F – left hand F,C,G,A). The right hand can continue to improvise using exclusively white notes.

7. For chord two, D minor, the left hand can play D, A, E, and F. This chord can similarly follow the chord of C, or the chord of F, or the chord of A minor.

For these first seven steps, the right hand has only played white notes. We are now going to move on to a different sound – the Lydian mode,

If we stay using the notes of C major scale, we can step up the white notes, one by one, from any C to another C an octave higher (note one of C major to the higher note one (or 8)) giving us a major scale, or we can step up the white notes from D (note 2 in C major) to the higher D (note 9 in C major), giving us mode 2 of C major , similarly we can find mode 3, mode 4, up to mode 7 (white notes running from B to B). These modes each have different names, for example mode 2 is the Dorian mode, and mode 3 is the Phrygian mode. We are now going to look at mode 4, which is called the Lydian mode.

Important. When we refer to a certain mode, the mode will always begin on the root of the mode. A G dorian will begin on G, similarly an E flat mixolydian will begin on E flat. So if I refer to a B Lydian, I am referring to a mode that begins on B. We find our mode by first finding the major scale starting on the same note as the root of the mode (e.g. for B lydian we would first find B major scale), and then altering it as required. In this case, to find B Lydian, we would find a B major scale and then raise the 4th. Similarly, to find a B mixolylian mode, we would first find a B major scale and then flatten the 7th. To find a B dorian we would first find a B major scale, and then flatten the 3rd and the 7th. This paragraph might not make sense at the moment, but if you get confused later, refer back to this and hopefully all will become clear.

The Lydian mode

Mode 4 of C major , white notes running from F to F, is also called F Lydian mode. If we compare this mode to an F major scale, which contains a B flat, we can see that the only difference is that the 4th degree of F major scale (the B flat) has been raised to a B natural. Knowing this, we know that we can find any Lydian mode we choose by finding the major scale and then raising the 4th degree.

For example: G major scale has one sharp, an F sharp. To convert G major scale to G Lydian we can raise the 4th degree, which will give us G, A, B, C sharp, D, E, F sharp and G. Here, we have raised the 4th degree, C, to a C sharp.

Exercise

Find C Lydian, then D Lydian, and then find E flat Lydian.

Film music including Lydian modes

From our chord of C major (left hand plays C, G, D, E), we can move to a B flat chord, using a B flat Lydian in our right hand. Now the left hand will play B flat, F, C, and D, from the bottom up, in flowing quavers, and the right hand will play notes from B flat Lydian, i.e. B flat, C, D, E, F, G, A. We can improvise freely using these notes, and then we can return to the chord of C. Similarly, we can move from C to A flat, using A flat Lydian, then back to C.

Film music step 8

8. C can move to B flat. In B flat, the left hand can play **B flat, F, C, D**, while the right hand plays B flat Lydian. This is B flat major scale with a raised 4th – B flat, C, D, E, F, G, A, B flat. The only black note is B flat. We can improvise in B flat Lydian for a few bars before returning to C. Notice how the right hand set of notes has to agree with the left hand set; in this case we have introduced a B flat in the left hand, so we have to introduce a B flat in the right hand. We can change freely between our C chord and our B flat chord.

9. C can also move an A flat chord. In A flat, the left hand will play **A flat, E flat, B flat and C**, in flowing quavers from the bottom up, while the right hand improvises using A flat Lydian – A flat, B flat, C, D, E flat, F, G and A flat. We can stay in A flat Lydian for a few bars before returning to C. Again, we can move freely between our C chord and our A flat chord.

Film music incorporating a raised 5th (C+)

10. C+. From C, we can make an interesting change. The fifth of the triad of C is the note G; if we raise this to a G sharp we get the left hand figure C, G sharp, D, E. We have to accommodate this G sharp in our right hand notes, and if we experiment, we find that we can use a G in the right hand, and we can use a G sharp, but we can't use an A – it sounds horrid. With this in mind, for our right hand notes we will use C, D, E, F, G, G sharp, B, and C. Playing in this raised fifth mode gives a wonderful bitter-sweet sound, which will resolve happily to C. Alternatively, we could go on to a C chord with a 6 in it, which is what we will look at in stage 11.

11. **C6**. From the C with a raised 5th that we found in step 10, can go to a C chord with a 6th. The left hand G sharp (of C with raised 5th) can rise a semitone to A, so the left hand will play C, A, D, E. The right hand can return to using any white notes, since the left hand is only using white notes.

12. **C7**. From C with a 6th, we can move to a C7 chord. The A in the left hand C6 chord can move up another step to B flat, so the left hand will now play C, B flat, D, E. The right hand has to accommodate the B flat in the left hand, so it will play a mode C, D, E, F, G, A, B flat, and C. This is actually called C Mixolydian mode - it differs from the C major scale in that it has a flattened 7th (B flat).

13. From C7 we can move to the chord of F as described in step 4, then we can move back to C. Alternatively, having moved from C 7 to the chord of F, we might move to F minor. For **Fm**, (F minor) the left hand can play F, C, G, A flat, while the right hand plays F, G, A flat, B flat, C, D, E, F. This can resolve back to C

Steps 10 to 13 form a nice sequence,| C |C+ |C6 |C7 |F |Fm |C|. Each chord might be played for several bars before moving on to the next chord.

We will now look at the minor modes, using our film music improvisation as a tool to assist this exploration.

If you have played any scales and/or arpeggios for classical exams, you will know that the big difference between the major sound and the minor sound is the lowered third of the minor chord. For example, C major chord consists of C, E, and G, but C minor chord consists of C E flat and G. The third is the note which governs whether the chord is major or minor. But when you played these minor scales, you might have learned a number of other differences: for example, when you learned C minor, you might have learned that C harmonic minor had an E flat and also an A flat. You might also have learned C melodic minor, which only has E flat going up but has B flat, A flat and E flat going down. Notice that the third, i.e., the E flat, remains constant, but the 6th and 7th degrees may be raised or lowered.

14. We can move from C major directly to C minor, provided that the right hand is not on an E or E flat while the left hand is changing. The notes for the left hand in C minor are C, G, D, E flat. While the left hand is playing this, the right hand can explore some minor modes. The right hand can experiment and can explore:

    1. Notes used in C melodic minor ascending – C, D, E flat, F, G, A, B, C.

       Notice that this is C major scale with a flattened 3rd.

    2. C Dorian - C, D, E flat, F, G, A, B flat, C.

       Notice that this is C major scale with a flattened 3rd and flattened 7th.

    3. Notes used in C melodic minor descending – C, D, E flat, F, G, A flat, B flat, C. This mode is in fact called the C Aolian mode. Also it is called C natural minor.

       Notice that this is C major scale with flattened 3rd, 7th, and 6th.

    4. C harmonic minor - C, D, E flat, F, G, A flat, B, C.

    5. Having explored these four minor modes, we can see that the E flat stays put, but the A and the B are altered freely. Altering the A and B as many times as you like, freely experiment as you improvise in the minor. You might even play on a melodic descending mode as you ascend, and a melodic ascending mode as you descend, because this feels curiously rebellious!

C minor will freely move back to C major, provided that the right hand avoids the E/E flat as you change the left hand.

This film music sequence is very useful, because in the process of learning it you have covered many important modes, including the Lydian, Mixolydian, Dorian, and other minor modes. When you practice this piece, you can move freely from one section to another, and this will help build your ability to navigate around various sounds at the keyboard.

Lesson Seven:
Shells

One of the big challenges in playing jazz is getting a sound out of the piano which sounds 'complete' to the listener. A number of great jazz pianists, for example Bud Powell, frequently use a minimalistic technique where the left hand only plays two notes per chord as the right hand improvises. As we will see when we study harmony, the most important notes in a chord are the root, the 3rd, and the 7th. Shells consist of the root at the bottom, and EITHER the 3rd or the 7th at the top. To get us started we will limit ourselves to playing the root at the bottom and the 7th at the top. These shells only sound good in the pitch range between middle C and the F which is an octave and a bit below it. If they are played any lower, the sound becomes very muddy, if they are played higher, they lose their supportive quality. To find a shell with the 7th at the top, play the root at the bottom of the left hand and reach up an octave. Now move your thumb down two steps (semitones) and this will be your 7th. For example for a C7 chord your left hand would play C at the bottom and B flat at the top.

Exercise

Find an F7 chord, and a G7 chord in this way (shell form).

Now play around with the shells of C7, F7, and G7, playing the following sequence over and over again. Be sure to count the 4 beats to every bar (hold each shell for 4 beats).

|C7 | F7 | C7| C7 |

|F7 | F7 |C7 | C7 |

|G7 |F7 |C7 | C7 |

To help you out, for F7 shell your left hand should have an F at the bottom and E flat at the top, and for G7 shell you should have G at the bottom and F at the top.

When you feel ready, add some C blues ideas in your right hand. Blues scale work was described at the end of lesson four, where we used a descending left hand idea (C, B flat, A flat, G) to support our right hand blues scale improvisation. Now that we have discovered shells, we can also support this same right hand blues work by going around the blues chord sequence (blues progression) in the shells above. Make sure that the bars are all the same length and the pulse is even and regular. Drum some swing rhythms before you play this so that you can produce an improvisation that is rhythmically good - the timekeeping aspect is one of the biggest challenges here.

Lesson Eight:
Blue Monk - our first jazz piece

Now that the student will have some facility and is able to improvise, we can play a short jazz standard. The left hand is playing 'shells' here, as described above, these consisting of two notes —the root at the bottom and the 7th at the top.

Either by copying from a performance on the internet or by using a copy of the music, learn the tune for 'Blue Monk' by Thelonius Monk in the key of C. To support your tune use shells in the left hand. Notice how full the left hand shells sound. Aim to get a jazzy swing, don't worry if you can't quite manage the quirky timing of the piece.

Keeping in time, play the piece slowly, but swinging, a few times, until you have 'got the hang' of it (can you memorise it?). Concentrate on making it swing, using the rhythm work you have done, and remember to keep the speed down for now. Also, remember that if you try to do too much in the right hand you will lose the swing feel, so really focus on that 'bluesy sound'.

You can now play the melody and a short solo. A Jazz musician will play a melody, then they will play a few solos, then they will play the melody again to finish off with. You can do this now, using the work from the previous lesson (C blues in right hand over a left blues sequence in shells) as your solo section. You can now perform your first jazz tune!

When soloing, remember that if you try to do too much in the right hand you will lose the swing feel, so keep the number of notes down , keep your musical pulse strong, and really focus on that 'bluesy swing' sound.

Lesson Nine:
Let's start some harmony

We have now developed a bit of keyboard skill, and we can sit down and improvise, so we are ready to look at some harmony. We want to develop an understanding of chords within the jazz 'nomenclature'.

The minor 7 chord is an extension of the minor triad, adding a 7th above the 5th. This means that if we find our minor triad, all we need to do is to find the 7th, and we found a technique for finding a 7th when we looked at shells. You find the triad, and if you find a root (8th) on top of this, you can find the 7th by counting down two semitones. For example, on top of a C minor triad I could find a C, and then I could count down two steps to find the 7th, B flat. So the notes for C minor 7 would be:

C, E flat, G, and B flat.

Exercise:

Find a G minor 7 chord, then find and F minor 7 chord, then go on to find three more minor 7 chords.

Comparing the C minor 7th chord with the C blues scale, see how the notes for the blues scale are almost the same as for the minor 7th chord, the difference being the addition of the 4th and the raised 4th. Because the blues scale contains all of the notes of the minor 7 chord, we can improvise in C blues over C minor 7. Similarly we can do this in any key, for example, over F sharp minor 7th chord we could use an F sharp blues.

Exercise:

Using C minor 7 in the left hand, improvise in the right hand using C blues scale. Experiment using funk, latin, swing or any other style you can find.

Exercise:

Find a few random minor 7 chords (1,3,5,7 = the minor triad with a 7th on top) in the left hand, and find the associated blues scale in the right hand, and then make up a short piece. Notice how any minor7 chord can move to any other minor7 chord (moving in parallel). It might help to start off with some easily found chords and scales, for example D minor 7 is all white notes (D,F,A,C) and D blues uses the same notes as this chord, with the addition of G and G sharp. Maybe choose G minor 7 and F minor 7 along with C minor 7, and string these together in any order you wish.

We can also find a basic **7th chord**, 1, 3, 5, 7 = major triad with 7th on top (e.g. C7 = C, E, G, Bflat) and we can find **major 7th chords**, 1, 3, 5, 7, = major triad with major 7th on top. (e.g. C maj7 = C, E, G, <u>B</u> similarly G major7 = G, B, D, <u>Fsharp</u>) The major 7th is only *one step/semitone below* the upper root, hence my underlining.

Exercise:

Find basic 1, 3, 5, 7, voicings for F7, G7, A7, Bflat7, and then find basic 1, 3, 5, 7, voicings for F major7, A major7, and E flat major 7.

Finding a minor 9th chord

Having found a C minor 7 chord, we can also add a 9th above the 7th, giving us a C minor 9 chord. I.e., going up from the root C we have: C, E flat, G, B flat, and D.

Notice that the 7th and 9th are a tone (two semitones = two steps) each side, i.e., above and below, the root.

When we play in a jazz band, we will usually have a bass player who will be playing the root of the chord for us – this means that we can leave out the roots when we play our chords, playing the 3rd and 7th, and maybe some other notes, but leaving the roots for the bass player to play. Similarly, if we are playing jazz in a duo without a bass player, our left hand will play the roots, so our right hand can find chords with no root.

This means that playing alone at the piano, when we play a chord, the right hand may play 3,5,7 and 9, while the left hand plays the root (1). Alternatively, if we have a bass player, he/she can play the root, while we can play 3,5,7 and 9 in the left hand, leaving our right hand completely free to improvise. This 3,5,7,9 chord is a standard jazz voicing which you will hear many times in almost any jazz performance, and it has an inversion which is equally popular and serves the same purpose. This is the 7, 9, 3, 5, voicing. Let me explain.

If we take 3 and 5 to the top of the chord, we have another good jazz sound, a 7, 9, 3, 5 voicing. For example, for C minor, our 3, 5, 7, 9, voicing is E flat, G, B flat, D, and if we move 3 and 5 (= E flat and G) to the top, we will get a 7, 9, 3, 5 voicing, (B flat, D, E flat and G). I will set out a series of steps for you to follow which will both talk you through finding this chord and help you to understand the theory:

1. Find a C minor 9 chord, C, E flat, G,B flat, D. (=1,3,5,7,9)

2. Leave out the root (1), leaving you with E flat, G, B flat, D. (=3,5,7,9).(You could play a bass root(C) in the left hand, an octave or two below the rest of the chord.)

3. Keeping the B flat and the D (7 and 9) in place, take both the E flat and the G (3 and 5) up an octave.

4. This will leave you with B flat, D, E flat and G, which is a 7,9,3,5, voicing for C minor9. (Bottom upwards).

5. The chord you have found is probably an octave too high. Move this entire chord down an octave so that you are playing it in the middle range of the keyboard, i.e., you will have middle C between your B flat (=7)and D (=9).

A shortcut to find the 7,9,3,5 voicing for a minor 7th chord

As mentioned before, 7 and 9 are a tone either side of the root, so from our C minor triad we have a shortcut we can use to find this voicing.

1. Find a C minor triad. C, E flat, G.

2. Replace the C with the 7th (two steps below C(= B flat)) and the 9th (two steps above C (= D) i.e., we have replaced the bottom note of the triad with notes a tone each side.

3. You should now have B flat, D, E flat and G. This is a 7,9,3,5, voicing for Cminor9.

...in brief, find a minor triad, then keeping the top two notes (=3 and 5) in place, substitute the bottom note (root) for notes two steps (= one tone) each side.

Find 7,9,3,5 voicings for C minor, F minor, G minor and a few more of your own choice. It is a good idea to play the 7,9,3,5 voicing in your right hand while your left hand plays the root. You might choose to make up a rhythm between the hands. These chords sound good, so enjoy them.

NB – these chords are generally played in the middle range of the keyboard, middle C lying somewhere between the top and bottom notes.

We can compose a short piece using these chords by adding a funky bass line, giving us a typical dance music track. Taking as a reference point the root of each chord as we play it, we can approach each (LH) root in semitone steps from a tone (=2 steps) below. For example, for our C minor chord the left hand could play B flat – B – C. For this piece use C, F, and G minor 7,9,3,5 voicings in the right hand, while the left hand provides a funky bass line - improvise a short piece.

You can add other minor 7,9,3,5 chords in other keys to the piece. Have a play!

Another improvisation

Using the descending left hand figure we learned when we studied the blues scale (root – down two steps – down two steps – down one step, e.g. in C we would play C – Bflat – Aflat – G, all played two beats per note) we can practise a right hand improvisation that switches between blues scale and minor 7,9,3,5 chords. We can explore lots of strange keys in this way, first finding the left hand descending figure, then, while the left hand continues, finding the minor triad in the right hand and going around the notes in the triad, then adding the flattened 5th and the note below this (=4), then finding the upper root and the note two steps below this (=7th). This gives the complete blues scale, which can alternate with minor 7,9,3,5 chords.

This way we can build up and learn all the blues scales and minor 7,9,3,5 chords WHILE we play.

Lesson Ten:
Major 7 chords

Working in the scale of C major, which is exclusively white notes, we can play a major triad and extend it by playing a major 7th and (ordinary) 9th on top, giving us C, E,G,B,D. Notice how the 7th (B) is only a **semitone** (single step) below the higher C.

Our left hand (or bass player) can play the root (C) an octave or two lower, so we can leave our root out. Now we have a nice voicing for a C major chord (3,5,7,9 = E, G, B, D).

As before with minor 7 chord voicings, this can be re-arranged to form a 7,9.3,5 voicing, the difference being that now we have a major 3rd and major 7th.

We can again use a shortcut to find this chord. Find a major triad (1,3,5), then replace the root (1) with major 7(down semitone from root) and 9 (up tone from root). See below for a step by step explanation.

A shortcut to find the major chord in 7, 9, 3, 5, voicing

As when we found the minor version of this chord, we can do this in any key. Here is the process for a C major chord:

1. Find a C major triad. C, E, G (=1,3,5).
2. Replace the C (=1) with the major 7th (one step below C(= B)) and the 9th (two steps above C (=D))
3. You should now have B, D, E and G. This is a 7,9,3,5, voicing for Cmajor9

...in brief, find the major triad, then replace the bottom note of this triad with notes one step (semitone) below and two steps (a tone) above.

Find 7.9, 3, 5, voicings for F maj7, Eflat Maj7, Aflat Maj7 and G maj7

Find a few more of these 7,9,3,5 major9 chords and make up a short composition, playing the chords in your right hand while your left hand plays the roots.

N.B. These are Major 9th chords. When we play jazz , we can freely extend 7th chords to become 9th chords , so when we refer to a chord such as D minor 7, we might in fact be choosing to play a D minor 9. I will be offering extended voicings in the place of ordinary 7th chords in this manner throughout the book, so be aware of this when I discuss the 2-5-1 progression and thereafter.

Improvisation using C and F major chords in 7,9,3,5 voicing

Playing the roots in octaves in the left hand (maybe holding the bottom of these two left hand notes down while the top note is re-iterated), we can move between C and F major chords in 7,9,3,5 voicing and generate a rock groove. In between these chords we can improvise on the white notes using single lines of notes and 6ths.**A free improvisation**

If our left hand plays a major triad with a major 7th on top, giving us C, E, G, B,(= the chord of C major 7th voiced 1, 3, 5, 7,)), we have a complete sound which we can use to support an improvisation in the right hand. Play this chord, C major 7th, in your left hand now. The right hand can improvise over this. Because all the notes of the major 7 chord are notes in the C major scale, we can use the notes from C major scale as a set of notes available to the improviser. Experiment with this now, using swing rhythm.

Another scale option for the improviser (over the left hand major 7th chord) is the LYDIAN mode. This is a major scale with a raised 4th that we discussed when we learned our 'Film Music' improvisation. Find B flat Lydian, then A flat Lydian, along with the major 7th chords in 1, 3, 5, 7, voicing for these keys. Now using a swing rhythm, experiment playing a (LH) C major 7 chord with a (RH) C major scale improvisation on top, then move to a B flat major 7 chord with a B flat Lydian over the top, then to an A flat major7 chord with an A flat Lydian over the top. Move freely around these three chords. Experiment now, adding other major 7 chords and improvising over them in the appropriate Lydian modes.

Notice how a major 7 chord can freely move to any other major 7 chord (moving in parallel), and notice how the Lydian mode is less stable than the major scale, making it easy to switch to other keys because it has less 'gravitational pull'.

Also this might help if you want to explore 3,5,7,9 voicings.

To find any minor 3,5,7,9.

- Find a minor triad in your left hand somewhere close to middle C. (1,3,5)

- Right hand plays notes two steps each side of the upper root – the root above the triad. (7,9)

- Bottom note of the left hand triad (1) moves down a couple of octaves to provide a low root, while right hand holds on to the notes it has (7,9) and takes over the top two notes of the left hand's minor triad (3,5).

- The right hand now has the minor 3,5,7,9 voicing.

To find any major 3,5,7,9.

- Find a major triad in your left hand somewhere close to middle C. (1,3,5)

- Right hand plays a note one step below the upper root, and two steps above the upper root. (Major 7th and 9th)

- Bottom note of the left hand triad (1) moves down a couple of octaves to provide a low root, while right hand holds on to the notes it has (7,9) and takes over the top two notes of the left hand's major triad (3,5).

- The right hand now has the major 3,5,7,9 voicing.

Lesson Eleven

The 2-5-1 in a major key.

This is a sequence of three chords that occurs very often. If we practise this sequence we are effectively practising three different types of chord in the order they are most likely to occur. A professional jazz pianist will play these chords in the left hand while the right hand improvises on top (bass player plays the roots of the chords), but the best way to learn the chords is to play them in the right hand while the left hand plays the roots, because this enables us to relate all the notes in the right hand chord to the root in the left hand.

First, a little revision. If we are working in the key of C major (all white notes on the piano), we can build chords on each degree of the scale. Starting at the bottom of the scale, and building up triads using only the notes of C major scale, the first chord would be C major (chord 1), next chord D minor (chord 2), next chord E minor (chord 3), then F major (chord 4) then G major (chord 5) and so on (A minor chord 6, B diminished chord 7) up to the C major chord at the top (chord 1 again).

Exercise:

Without looking back at the paragraph above, what is chord 2 of C major scale? What is chord 4? What is chord 5? Look back to check your answers.

Working in the key of G major, we will be using the notes G, A, B, C, D, E, F sharp, and G. Because there is an Fsharp in the G Major scale, any F's will become F sharps. In this scale, G major will be chord 1, A minor will be chord 2, B minor will be chord 3 etc. Attempt the following exercise.

Exercise:

What is chord 2 in G major? What is chord 5 in G major?

And then moving to other keys: What is chord 2 in F major? What is chord 5 in F major? What is chord 2 in B flat major? What is chord 3 in B flat major? What is chord 5 in B flat major?

Answers, in G major, chord 2 is A minor, chord 5 in G is D major, and then in F major chord 2 is G minor, chord 5 is C major, and finally in B flat major, chord 2 is C minor, chord 3 is D minor and chord 5 is F major.

The 2 – 5 – 1 progression is a progression of chord 2 to chord 5 then to chord 1. In many jazz pieces we find the 2-5-1 progression occurring in abundance. For example, in a piece in the key of C major we will be very likely to find the progression Dm7 – G7 – C maj7. Often we have the complete progression, but frequently we may have the 2-5 part of the progression, and then we might dive to some other chord. For example, the tune Ladybird has Fm7 – B flat7 – C maj7; on this occasion we have a 2-5 progression in E flat major (Fm7 = chord 2 in E flat, B flat 7 is chord 5) but then we dive to C major after our chord 5.

Indentifying the 2 - 5 - 1

Notice that in a major scale, chord 2 is a minor 7th chord. Also notice that the second note of the major scale, i.e. the root of chord 2, is two steps (= a tone) above the start note of the major scale (key note). Similarly, chord 5 is a 7th chord which is based a fifth above the start note of the major scale. Chord 1, the chord of the starting note of the major scale, is a major 7th chord. The notes that identify these chords are the **root**, the **third** (3rd), and the **seventh** (7th). I will explain.

1. Chord 2: minor 7th. This has a minor third, and the 7th is down two steps below its root. For example, D minor will have F (=minor 3rd) and C (down 2 steps).

2. Chord 5: 7th chord. This has a major 3rd, and the 7th is down two steps below its root. For example, G7 will have B (=major 3rd) and F (down 2 steps).

3. Chord 1: major 7th. This has a major 3rd, but the 7th is only one step below its root. For example, C major 7 will have E (=major 3rd) and B (down 1 step).

So we see that the third and the seventh govern whether the chord is major or minor, and also govern the type of seventh.

We can add other notes to these chords, but so long as the root is at the bottom and the third and

7th are present, the chord identity is secure. The 3rd and 7th can swap positions, i.e., the 3rd may be above the 7th, as it was when we found the 7, 9, 3, 5, voicings.

Jazz voicings for the 2 - 5 – 1 progression

In the key of C major, chord 1 will be C major and chord 2 will be D minor. These chords can be extended, and we can replace simple triads and basic 7th chords with the more interesting 7,9,3,5 voicings we have looked at. Our chord 1, C major, will be B,D,E,G while left hand plays the root C, and our chord 2, D minor, will be C,E,F,A, while the left hand plays a D.

Chord 5 will be a G7 chord in C major. Here is a shortcut to find a chord 5 after a chord 2. This is shown for C major, but can be applied to any major key.

Easier way to find notes to form a 2 – 5 progression in a major key (described for key of C major)

Find a 7,9,3,5 voicing for D minor (in your right hand), left hand plays the root (D). This will be C,E,F,A. running bottom to top.

Now, keeping all the other chord notes in place, move your right hand thumb down a single semitone (one step). As you play the new chord with your right hand thumb one step lower, your left hand plays the root of chord 5 (G). Play the new root and new chord together, this is now the chord G7 – we have moved from chord 2 to chord 5. Left hand is playing the root G, and the right hand has the chord B, E, F, A, (3, 6, 7, 9), which contains the 3rd and 7th for G7, thus it is an identifiable G7 chord.

This technique of finding a chord 2 in 7, 9, 3, 5 voicing and moving our right hand thumb down to access chord 5 gives us a shortcut from chord 2 to chord 5, and it works in any major key.

In effect , by moving the thumb down a semitone within our chord 2 (D minor 7, 9, 3, 5), we have found a 3,6,7,9 voicing for G7 – B, E, F, A.

We know that in relation to G7 the chord has the correct 3rd and 7th, i.e. major 3rd and the 7th is down 2 steps below the root, (B and F), so if the root is provided by the left hand (G), we will have an identifiable G7 chord, and we know that G7 is chord 5 of C major scale.

From the D minor7, (C, E, F, A), we have moved our C down a step to the B. Notice how, as we have mentioned, the chord 2 is a minor 7th chord and the chord 5 is a 7th chord.

NB: In classical music theory, any 7th which is down 2 steps from the root is actually called a minor 7th. I refer to this minor 7th as 'down 2 steps' to avoid confusion.

The complete 2 – 5 – 1 in a major key

Having found the 2 - 5, we can put a chord 1 (C major 7th in this case) on the end to get a 2-5-1 progression.

So our three chords are:

1. Chord 2. D minor7 = C,E,F,A.
2. Chord 5. G7 = B,E,F,A
3. Chord 1. C major7 = B,D,E ,G.

We now know that we can find a 7, 9, 3, 5 voicing for a chord 2 (=min7 chord), then we can drop our right hand thumb to find our chord 5 (=7th chord) then we can find our chord 1 (= major 7 chord). We can apply this to any key we choose. For example, in G major the full progression would be Amin7 – D7 – Gmajor7. We would find a 7, 9, 3, 5 voicing for Amin7, then to find D7 the right hand thumb would move down a step (from G to F sharp), then we would find chord 1 (G major 7 in a 7, 9, 3, 5 voicing). Watch out for the F sharp in the right hand at the bottom of the D7 and G maj7 chords.

Exercise:

Find voicings for a 2-5-1 in G major, F major, B flat major, E flat major, and then other random keys. Learn these chords and play a latin rhythm as you practise them. If you play a series of 2 – 5 – 1 progressions moving down in tones, e.g., in G, then in F, then in E flat, we have a smooth progression where the each chord 1 will move to a chord 2 in the next key which has the same root. For example, the chord 1 of G (G major 7) smoothly changes to G minor 7 as it changes to become chord 2 in F major. Help is on the next page!

To help you get started, a 2 – 5 – 1 in …

1. G major = A min7 (use thumb down to reach) D7 then find Gmaj7.

2. F Major = G min7 to C7 to F maj7.

3. E flat major = F min7 to B flat7 to E flat maj7.

   To help you get started: in F major, chord 2 is G minor (F, A, B flat, D) then chord 5 is C7 (E, A, B flat, D), and then chord 1 is F major (E, G, A, C).

Briefly, in order to find a major 2-5-1 you

1. Find chord 2. Find the (minor) triad of chord 2, then replace the bottom note with notes two steps each side.

2. Find chord 5. Keeping all other notes in place, lower the bottom note of chord 2 one step. This will provide chord 5.

3. Find chord 1. Find the (major) triad of chord 1, then replace the bottom note with notes one step below and two steps above.

   Chords are played in the right hand (for now) while left hand plays the roots of the chords.

In the next lesson we will see how sometimes a piece of music can be built almost entirely on 2 - 5 progressions and major chords.

Assistance for the 2-5-1 progression

This is a section I inserted because many students were having trouble with this progression. I hope that this insertion will be helpful.

Firstly, the purpose of this is to learn three different types of chords in the order they most frequently occur.

1. Chord 2 is a minor7 chord in 7,9,3,5 voicing. The root of chord 2 is the second note of the major scale, which is two steps above the root of chord 1. For example, in the key of C major the root of chord 2 will be two steps above C, which is the note D. This will be a minor7 chord, i.e. D minor7 in 7,9,3,5 voicing.

Similarly, chord 2 in G major will be A minor7 (A is two steps above G), and chord 2 in F major will be G minor7. Getting a bit more complicated, chord 2 of B flat major will be C minor, and chord 2 of F sharp major will be G sharp minor.

To find the minor 7,9,3,5 voicing, find the minor triad in your right hand and replace the bottom note (root) with notes two steps each side, while the left hand plays a low root.

2. Chord 5 is a 7th chord in 3,6,7,9 voicing, which is found simply by keeping the top three notes of chord 2 in place while the bottom note goes down one step (all right hand). I refer to this as 'the thumb-down trick', because the thumb moves down one note. The left hand plays the root, which is note 5 of the major scale. This is 7 steps above the starting note of the scale, or 5 steps above the root of chord 2. For example, in the key of C major the root of chord 5 will be G.

3. Chord 1 is a major chord in 7,9,3,5 voicing based on the starting note of the scale, i.e. in the key of C it will be a C major 7th chord in 7,9,3,5 voicing. Similarly in G major, chord 1 will be a G major chord in 7,9,3,5.

To find the major 7,9,3,5 voicing, find the major triad in your right hand and replace the bottom note (root) with notes one step below and two steps above. Left hand plays a low root.

The thumb-down trick is useful for finding a 7th chord that follows a minor 7th chord in a 2-5 pattern, but it only works when finding a 7th chord. When you study Misty, be sure that the only time you use the thumb-down trick is when you are finding the 7th chords.

When learning these chords it is probably most helpful to go through a piece learning all the minor 7th chords, then the major 7th chords, then joining them together with the 7th chords using the thumb-down trick wherever you can spot a 2-5-1 (or 2-5) progression.

Another helpful tip: When finding a minor triad it will be 3 steps between the bottom two notes and 4 steps between the top two. Similarly, when finding a major triad it will be 4 steps between the bottom two notes and 3 steps between the top two. In both cases the two numbers add up to 7.

Lesson Twelve:
Play Misty for me

This piece is full of 2-5 progressions. In fact, whenever there is a minor 7th chord followed by a 7th chord there is a 2 - 5 pattern. This means that we can find the chord for the minor 7th and simply change the bottom note to find the 7th chord which follows. There are also two major 7th chords, E flat major and A flat major, which we can find in 7, 9, 3, 5 voicings, as we did when we looked at major chords this voicing. Also, watch out for the two consecutive minor 7th chords, C minor 7, which moves to F minor 7, in the second line (and last line). When playing these chords, you will have to find each chord separately. **The thumb down trick only works when we move from minor 7th chord to 7th chord**. This piece will take some time to learn, but when it has been learned, you will have learned many commonly used chords, which can be used for other jazz pieces. One such jazz piece being 'Ladybird', which is a good tune to study after Misty because it shares many of the chords, although the tempo is faster, so the piece lends itself to an up-tempo swing. I will give you the chord sequences to both pieces. You might choose to team up with a saxophone player, who could play the melody over your chords, but the chords sound pleasant on their own too. While the RH plays the chords, the LH plays the roots.

To play Misty, first find all of the min7 chords in 7, 9, 3, 5, voicings, (B flat min 7, A flat min 7, F min 7, C min 7, G min 7, A min 7)then, where these are followed by 7th chords, the chord is found simply by moving the thumb down a semitone. Having found these 2 – 5 progressions, you could then find the major7 chords (there are only two, E flat major7 and A flat major7), remembering that the major 7th note itself is only down a semitone. Also, remember to find the C minor – F minor chords individually where they occur next to each other in the second, fourth, and last lines.

Misty

|E flat maj7	|B flat min7 Eflat7	|A flat maj7	| A flat min7 Dflat7 |
|E flat maj7 C min7	|F min7 B flat7	|Gmin7 C7	|F min7 B flat7 |
|E flat maj7	|B flat min7 Eflat7	|A flat maj7	| A flat min7 Dflat7 |
|E flat maj7 C min7	|F min7 B flat7	|E flat maj7 A flat maj7	|E flat maj7 |
|B flat min7	|E flat7	|A flat maj7	| A flat maj7 |
|A min7 D7	|C min7 F7	|Gmin7 C7	|F min7 B flat7 |
|E flat maj7	|B flat min7 Eflat7	|A flat maj7	| A flat min7 Dflat7 |
|E flat maj7 C min7	|F min7 B flat7 |	E flat maj7 A flat maj7	|E flat maj7

Ladybird

|C maj7		C maj7	|F min7		B flat7	
	C maj7		C maj7		B flat min7		E flat7	
	A flat maj7		A flat maj7		A min7		D7	
	Dmin7		G7		C maj7 Eflat7		A flat maj7 Dflat7	

Notice that in the last two bars of ladybird we have E flat7 and D flat7, which we cannot find simply by putting our thumb down a semitone because they are not preceded by a chord 2, so we have to remember them from when we played them in Misty, and then play them from memory – or look ahead to the section on 7th chords (next section). Finding these last three chords is actually very difficult, so although I suggest that you learn them, I recommend that if you choose to perform this with a sax player you just play the LH roots (leave out these last three RH chords in performance).

More about the 7th chord – how to find it without having to find a chord 2 first

Sometimes we have to find a 7th chord. We can already find this chord if it is in a 2-5-1 sequence, but how can we find it when it is standing alone?

We have established that in a major key, chord 2 is a minor7 chord and chord 1 is a major7 chord, and we have found out how to produce a 2 – 5 – 1 chord sequence, where we can find the chord 5 by altering our chord 2. Chord 5 is a 7th chord, and whereas this often serves as the middle chord in a 2 – 5 – 1 sequence, we sometimes find a 7th chord on its own. With this in mind, we will need to find a strategy to find the notes for this chord in isolation.

As mentioned earlier, the 7th chord has a major 3rd, and a 7th which is 2 steps (a tone) below the root. For the major7 and minor7 chords we have already worked out 7, 9, 3, 5 voicings, and we will soon move on to find 3, 5, 7, 9 voicings, but here we find that voicings for the 7th chord are slightly different. Rather than 3, 5, 7, 9, and 7, 9, 3, 5, we find that the 5th is replaced by a 6th. So for the 7th chord we will need to find a **7, 9, 3, 6** chord and a **3, 6, 7, 9** chord.

7th chord in 3, 6, 7, 9 voicing

1. Find the major triad, providing us with 1, 3, and 5. E.g, for C7 this would be C, E, G, from the bottom upwards.

2. From the root above this triad, find notes 2 steps below (providing the 7th of the chord) and 2 steps above (providing the 9th of the chord). This will give us a 1, 3, 5, 7, 9 voicing. E.g. for our C7 chord we would find the C above the triad and then find 2 steps below and two steps above, these notes will be B flat and D. With these notes on top of the triad we now have a 1, 3, 5, 7, 9 chord, which for C7 would be C, E, G, B flat and D.

3. The bass player, or the left hand in this case, will play the root (1) for us, so we can leave out the root, giving us a 3, 5, 7, 9 voicing, which will be E, G, B flat, and D for our C7 chord.

4. We replace the 5th with a 6th to give us our 3, 6, 7, 9 voicing, which is E, A, B flat, and D for C7. Notice that the 6th is just one step below the 7th. Also notice that the 6th is two steps above the 5th

Exercise

Find G7, F7, B flat, E flat7 and D7 in these voicings

Notice that this is the same type of chord as the middle chord in our 2 – 5 – 1. Test this by finding this voicing for G7, then F7, then B flat 7, and then compare these chords to the middle chords (the '5' chords) in your 2 – 5 – 1 sequences for C, B flat, and E flat majors respectively. They should be the same, and your G7 chord should be B, E, F, A from the bottom up, your F7 chord should be A, D, E flat, G, and your B flat 7 chord should be D, G, A flat, and C.

7th chord in 7, 9, 3, 6 voicing

1. Find the major triad (i.e. 1, 3, 5). E. g. for C7 you would find C, E, G, from the bottom upwards.

2. Replace the root with notes 2 steps either side (giving our 7th and 9th), this will provide a 7, 9, 3, 5 voicing. E.g. for C7, the C in your triad would be replaced by B flat and D, this will give us B flat, D, E, G, from the bottom upwards.

3. Replace the 5 with a 6. This will provide a 7, 9, 3, 6 voicing. For our C7 chord we will replace our 5 (G) with a 6 (A) this will give us B flat, D, E, A.

Exercise:

Find 7, 9, 3, 6 voicings for G7, F7, B flat7 E flat7 and D7. To help you get started, you should find that G7 is F, A, B, E, and that F7 is E flat, G, A, D, and that B flat 7 is A flat, C, D, G.

Compare these to the 3, 6, 7, 9 voicings of the same chords, noticing that the bottom two notes of one become the top two notes of the other. This 'note juggling' is a useful skill to acquire, so practice transforming one voicing of a chord into another.

Lesson Thirteen:
More about modes

A mode is a combination of notes at various intervals from each other, spanning an octave, and repeating the pattern every octave. It is a recursive pattern of notes. This means that the pattern repeats every subsequent octave as we go up the keyboard. One good example of a mode is the major scale, which is referred to as the 'Ionian' mode; here we have a pattern of notes which repeats every octave. If we are improvising using the notes in C major scale, all white notes on the piano, we can also find other modes simply by starting our scale on a different note. We discussed these ideas when we looked at our 'Film Music' improvisation, so feel free to refer back to this. Using only the notes of C major scale, which happen to be all white notes, we can run C to C which will give us a C major scale, or C Ionian mode, we can also run:

D to D. This gives us a Dorian mode (D Dorian). D Dorian is also referred to as mode 2 of C major. The Dorian mode can be found by finding the major scale, and then lowering the 3rd and 7th, so from D major scale (two sharps which are F and C), if we lower the 3rd (F sharp lowered to F natural) and 7th (C sharp lowered to C natural) we can find D Dorian.

1. E to E-Phrygian mode, or mode 3 C major scale. Comparing this set of consecutive white notes with E major scale (four sharps, which are F, C, G, and D) we notice that we can find E Phrygian from E major scale by lowering 2, 3, 6, and 7.

2. F to F- Lydian mode/ Mode 4 C major. F major scale raised 4th.

3. G to G -Mixolydian mode/Mode 5 C major. G major scale lowered 7th.

4. A to A –Aolian mode/Mode 6 C major. A major scale lowered 3, 6 and 7.

5. B to B Locrian mode/Mode 7 C major. B major scale lowered 2,3,5,6 and 7.

So,

When we play in any major scale, we can find a mode associated with each degree of that scale. These can be played over the chord associated with this degree. For example, over chord 2 we could play a mode 2 (Dorian), or over chord 5 we might play a mode 5 (Mixolydian). This is why we were able to play exclusively white notes in our 'Film Music' improvisation, where we played freely on C major triad (chord1), A min (chord6), F maj (chord4) and D min (chord2). Since all these chords relate to C major scale, our right hand can play exclusively white notes. The bass note determines the mode: for example, if we are using exclusively white notes and the bottom note is F we are working in F Lydian, or if the bass note is an E we are working in E Phrygian.

Similarly, when we play a 2 – 5 – 1 progression, we can improvise in the scale that all these chords relate to. For example, in the key of C major, the 2 -5 -1 progression is D min7 – G7 – Cmaj7, and we can play any notes from C major scale over any of these chords. Likewise, if we had a 2 -5 -1 in F major (G min7 –C7 – F maj7) we could play any notes from F major scale over any of these chords.

Having seen how we can play any of the notes of the relevant major scale over a 2-5-1 progression, let us see how we might apply this to a piece of music. You could attempt an improvisation, using notes from the appropriate scale in the right hand, while the left hand plays a rocking bass figure. This rocking bass figure can consist entirely of roots. For example, for the first chord C in bar one, the bass figure could be four equal beats, a low C, a C up an octave, low C again, then up the octave again. Alternatively, the left hand bass could consist of one long root for each bar, for example the left hand would play a single low C for the first bar, another low C for the second bar, and an F for the third bar. The aim of this task is to play a bass line and to improvise a solo on top.

Ladybird

|C maj7 |C maj7 |F min7 | B flat7 |

[C major scale to fit C major chord]   [E flat major scale-these are chords 2&5 in E flat major]

|C maj7 | C maj7 |B flat min7 |E flat7|

[C major scale][A flat major scale-this is a 2-5-1 progression in A flat]

|A flat maj7 |A flat maj7 |A min7 |D7 |

[Still A flat major]   [Gmajor scale-these are chords 2&5 in G major]

|Dmin7 |G7 |C maj7 Eflat7 |A flat maj7 Dflat7 |

[C major scale, chords 2&5 in C][C blues! Blues can be our default scale when things get complicated]

In addition to relating our 2 – 5 – 1 progressions to the associated scales, i.e. the maj scale of chord 1, we can also find the appropriate mode for each chord individually. We know that chord 2 is a minor 7 that takes a dorian mode, that chord 5 is a 7th chord which takes a mixolydian mode, and that chord 1 is a major 7 chord which takes a major scale, and so we can find the appropriate mode for each chord by finding the major scale starting on the mode's first note, and then altering the major scale in the ways we have discussed. For example D Dorian is D major scale with 3rd and 7th lowered. In the list of modes, we have described exactly how each mode differs from the major scale. We often have to find a mode without reference to a key, and in these cases it is always easier to find the mode starting by finding the major scale, and then altering the notes to find the mode.

Lesson Fourteen
Pentatonic scales, Improvisation in modes, and playing outside modes

The next pieces we will learn are great for developing fluent improvisation, and in addition they give the beginner an opportunity to experiment with the very modern sound produced by 'playing outside the mode'. The first two pieces are played on the white notes of the piano, so are relevant to C major scale, using mode 2 (D dorian) and mode 5 (G mixolydian). However, we might venture outside of these modes, meaning that we might include some black notes, for the effect of playing outside the mode.

As the notes of G Mixolydian and D Dorian modes consist exclusively of the white notes of the piano, the black notes of the piano are not included in the modes, and are said to be 'outside the mode'.

Pentatonic scales

The black notes form a **pentatonic** mode (Five note mode). Starting on G flat we have notes 1,2,3,5,6 in G flat major scale (G flat, A flat, B flat, D flat and E flat), this is called G flat **major pentatonic**. We can find the major pentatonic scale starting on any note by finding degrees 1,2,3,5,6 of the major scale. For example, C major pentatonic would consist of degrees 1,2,3,5,6 of C major scale, which will be C,D,E,G,A.

Exercise:

Find the major pentatonic modes for F, G, Eflat, and Aflat.

Using only black notes, starting on E flat, the black notes form E flat **minor pentatonic** (E flat, G flat, A flat, B flat, D flat) notice how the minor pentatonic scale is only one note different to the blues scale - if you add an A to E flat minor pentatonic you will have found an E flat blues scale. This can be used in reverse, - you can find your blues scale first then remove your flattened 5th to find the minor pentatonic.

Exercise

Find blues scales (lesson four) then remove the flat 5 to give minor pentatonic modes for C, F, A, and D.

Also notice that if you put down a minor 7 chord (1,3,5,7, which in C minor would be C, E flat, G, B flat) you can find the minor pentatonic by adding a 4 (1,3,4,5,7, which in C minor would be C, E flat, F, G, B flat), and again, from here you can find the blues scale by adding a flattened 5th to the pentatonic scale (which in C minor would be C, E flat, F, F sharp, G, B flat)

Funk and modern improvisations to play:

Mixolydian Funk

This piece is actually quite a challenge - if you can't manage it straight away, move on and come back to it later. It is a very exciting piece, and performing it can be made a lot easier by either playing over a recorded bass line or getting another person to play a bass line for you.

The piece is in G Mixolydian, and it gives you the opportunity to generate a piece primarily using rhythm at the piano. Additionally it gives us a chance to explore playing outside the mode we are working in. We can use a funky bass idea (left hand) and some modern sounding chords (based on stacks of 4ths) in the right hand.

It really helps to 'drive' this piece if you have someone else providing some funk drumming for you to play along to. Alternatively, you could use a basic drum machine to provide some sort of backing beat.

This piece is based in G Mixolydian, so we are using white notes (G major scale lowered 7th) and the bottom bass note is G.

For your bass line you can use the notes G, D, F and top G (bottom to top). Use these notes to make up a funky bass line. Play in a strong 4/4 at medium tempo, playing a low G at the start of each bar.

With your right hand play a G, and build a stack of 4ths on top (giving you G, C and F, bottom upwards). Play this chord over your left hand bass, and get a great funk 'groove' going.

Move this right-hand shape of 4ths around, using only white notes (for example, you could move to F,B,E or E, A, D etc). The 4ths will not all be perfect 4ths, but the 'shape' of the chord will stay the same as we move around inside the G mixolydian mode. Notice how freely you can move this shape (stack of 4ths). Because chords based on 4ths have no major or minor identity, they are highly mobile, and can move freely from one to another.

Now right hand again play the stack of 4ths (G, C, F) and this time take the top note F and move it down to the bottom of the chord (giving F, G, C) think of this as a 1,2,5 chord. Play this chord over the left hand funk riff, and when you feel ready, move the shape around the white notes as you did with the first (stack of 4ths) chord.

Now go back to the right hand stack of 4ths again (G, C, F) and take the bottom note G to the top, giving C, F, G. Think of this as a 1,4,5 chord and move this around in the same way as you moved the others.

Finally experiment with all three chords (all inversions of the stack of 4ths). Aim to get a driving funk groove. This is our basic Mixolydian funk groove. Really focus on the funk rhythm and generate a two handed funk groove.

Sometimes the right hand can stop playing chords and instead can improvise a line of single notes. We can alternate between chords and lines. Get your two hand funky bass and chord 'groove' going, then play a funky line of single notes with your right hand alone (all white notes) then return to the funk groove (bass and chords) with two hands, and switch between groove and solo line. At this point, you might like to work on the right hand soloing without the left hand. Remember the work on rhythm 1 **&**2 **&**3 **&**4 **&** and maybe include a 'Da ba do da' rhythm (accent the Da's) – notes played to the rhythm of the words.

Since all the white notes are 'inside' the mode, all of the black notes will be 'outside' the mode. This inside/outside phenomena can be used to great effect. When you do your right hand alone bit, left hand can stop playing altogether (or can continue) while your right hand plays lines of white notes, and then throw in a few strings of black notes for effect. Don't mix black and white, but play mostly white notes interspersed with little strings of black notes. Enjoy playing inside the mode and then slipping outside for a few notes (three or four ish) before returning to play inside again.

Dorian funk

Starting on D, we can find the D Dorian mode. Again, this is all white notes. We can treat this in exactly the same way as we treated the Mixolydian funk, using the same chords of stacked 4ths and the same 1,2,5 and 1,4,5 chords, only this time our bass notes will centre on the note D. We can include some 'so what' chords (called by this name because they first appeared in the jazz piece 'So What' by Miles Davis). Let's start by finding the D minor so what chord.

How to find a 'so what' chord

Here we find the so what chord in the keys of the original chords, D and E minor, but the technique can be used in order to find them in any key. For D minor:

1. Find a basic (1,3,5,7) D min7 chord (D,F,A,C). Use the notes in the region immediately below middle C, using your left hand.

2. Move the 3rd (F)and the 5th (A)up an octave and play them with your right hand. This will give you D, C, F, and A from the bottom upwards.

3. Fill in the gap above the root D (left hand) with the note a 4th above D (=G). This will leave you with a stack of 4ths (1,4,7,10) (D,G,C,F) with the 5th of the chord (A) on top. Giving D,G,C,F,A. This is the 'so what' voicing for D minor.

Having found your D minor so what chord, do the same for E min7. You should end up with E,A,D,G,B. We can use both of these chords freely in our Dorian funk.

Tip; Play the top three notes of these 'So What' chords in the right hand.

Using these chords, and supporting them with a bass 'D' (possibly with a preceding upbeat 'A') we can extend the piece, improvising on white notes when we are inside the mode and playing a few strings of black notes (outside the mode). Remember, in a 4/4 bar of swing, to emphasise the 'ands', 1 **&**2 **&**3 **&**4 **&**|1 **&**2 **&**3 **&**4 **&** etc. I suggest to my students that they play a swung set of quavers, DEFGAGFE|DEFGAGFE|DEFGAGFE accenting all the E's and G's, playing the D's, F's and A's much more quietly, then they can carry on using the rhythm throughout their improvisation. Be sure the notes are joined (Legato) They can also use a swung DACD accenting the D's, **dah** bah do **dah**, this rhythmic shape being used on various sets of notes inside the mode. The LH can support this with a selection of 'stacked 4ths' chords, 125 chords and 145 chords, maybe played the occasional low D.

Exercise

Find the so what chord for C minor 7, G minor 7, A minor, Eflat minor, and F minor 7.

The 'So what' chord can also be found like this:

1. Right hand find the minor triad, 1,3,5, (e.g. D,F,A for D minor) then replace the bottom note (=1=root which is the D in our D minor triad) with the note two steps below it (=7=C in our D minor example). This gives 7,3,5, which will be C,F,A in our example, going bottom to top.

2. Left hand find a root in the octave below (e.g. D for our D minor) then add a note a 4 th above it (=G in our D minor example).

3. From bottom of chord to top you should have the 'So what' chord, 1,4,7,3,5, which is D,G,C,F,A in our D min example.

Exercise

Use this method to find so what chords for A minor7, B minor7, and E minor7

A little more about playing outside the mode

The dorian and mixolydian modes provide a rich pool of resources for jazz players, and so there are many pieces written which give the improviser a long stretch of a single mixolydian or dorian mode. Because of this, these are the occasions when we are most likely to want to play outside the mode.

We have seen that in order to play outside a G mixolydian (white notes), we will play notes from G flat major pentatonic (black notes). This shows us that the notes outside the mixolydian mode (major scale with flattened 7th) form a major pentatonic starting a semitone below the start of the mixolydian mode. So if we wanted to find the notes outside a C mixolydian, we would find a B major pentatonic (= degrees 1,2,3,5,6 of B major scale).

Exercise

Find an F mixolydian , and then find the notes outside this mode. Move on to do the same for B flat mixolydian.

Similarly, we know that the notes outside a D dorian (Dorian mode equals major scale with flattened 3rd and 7th) will form a G flat major pentatonic (major pentatonic starting a **major 3rd** above the start of the dorian mode). So, if we were working in C dorian, we would find the 3rd degree of C major, which is E, then we would build an E major pentatonic in order to provide the notes outside the mode.

Exercise

Find a G dorian, and then find the notes outside it. Do the same for F dorian.

Another way to find notes outside the dorian mode

When we examined the pentatonic scale formed by the black notes, we found that we could either begin on G flat and produce a G flat major pentatonic (G flat, A flat, B flat, D flat, E flat), or we could start on E flat and produce E flat minor pentatonic (E flat, G flat, A flat, B flat, D flat), so we can see how the notes of the two pentatonic scales are shared, but the minor pentatonic begins a scale-note lower. Sometimes, when playing in the dorian mode, it is easier to find the minor pentatonic beginning a semitone above the start of the dorian mode.

For example, in D dorian (white notes) we would find E flat minor pentatonic (black notes).

As a general rule, this technique of finding the minor pentatonic starting a semitone above the root is particularly useful if you are playing in a complicated key. E.g., playing in F sharp dorian, we would find the outside notes by finding G minor pentatonic.

Exercise

Use this technique to find the notes outside A flat dorian; E dorian: and C sharp dorian.

Lesson Fifteen
The minor 2 – 5 – 1

The major 2 - 5 – 1 progression consists of three types of chord: a minor 7 chord, a 7th chord, and a major 7th chord. The 2 – 5 – 1 progression in a minor key has similarly three different chords. These are:

1. Chord 2 is a minor 7 chord with a flattened 5th. For this, we can play the 7, 9, 3, 5 voicing that we found before, from this chord we can flatten the 5th, the top note of this chord.

2. Chord 5 is a 7th chord with an altered 5th and 9th. This is sometimes called an altered chord, or an altered 7th. We will study one such chord, learning how to find a 7th chord with a sharpened 5th and a sharpened 9th.

3. Chord 1 is a minor chord. Along with adding a seventh and ninth as we did before when we found a 7, 9, 3, 5 voicing, we can add substitute the 7th for a 6th if we choose to. However, we will keep things simple for now and we will play the same 7, 9, 3, 5 voicing that we found for chord 2 in the major 2 – 5 - 1.

From this list, you can see that chords 2 and 1 are easily found by using techniques we have already learned. To recap: For chord 1, a minor 7th chord, we can find the minor triad then replace the bottom note with notes 2 steps each side (= a tone each side). For chord 2, a minor 7th chord with a flattened 5th, we find the minor triad, replace the bottom note with notes a tone each side, and then flatten the top note (which is the 5th of the chord). For example, for D minor 7 with a flattened 5th we can find our 7, 9, 3, 5, voicing, then we flatten the top note A to an A flat. This gives us C, E, F, A flat.

Exercise:

Find A minor7 flat5; Gminor7 flat 5; Fminor7 flat 5; B minor7 flat5; C minor7 flat5.

Having found our chord 2 and our chord 1, we are left with our chord 5, which is a 7th chord with sharpened 5th and 9th.

Finding a 7th chord with sharpened 5th and sharpened 9th

In 7, 9, 3, 5 voicing. Remember that the 7th chord is a chord with a major 3rd and a 7th which is down two steps (=a tone) from the upper root.

1. Find the major triad. For example, if we were finding G7 we would find G, B, D working from the bottom upwards.

2. Substitute the bottom note of the triad (= the root) for notes 2 steps either side – this provides our 7th and 9th. For example, in our G major triad we would substitute the G for F and A, giving us F,A,B, D, which is our 7th chord voiced 7, 9, 3, 5.

3. Sharpen the 9th and the 5th. For our G7 chord, this would give us F, A sharp, B, and D sharp.

Exercise:

Find 7th chords with sharpened 5th and 9th for C7, F7, Bflat7, and A7.

In 3, 5, 7, 9 voicing. We frequently have to find this same chord in a 3, 5, 7, 9 position. This is a little harder, but here is a technique to enable us to do this:

1. Find the major triad with your left hand. For example, for G7 we would find G, B, D.

2. On top of this triad, used your right hand to find the 7th and the 9th. These are two steps either side of the upper root. For our G7 example we would find the G above the triad and substitute it for notes two steps either side, giving us G, B, D, F, A from the bottom up.

3. Play the top four notes (3, 5, 7, 9, which are B, D, F, A in our example) with your right hand, while your left hand can move the root lower down. In our example the left hand would play a low G.

4. Sharpen the 5th and the 9th. This gives us B, D sharp, F , A sharp in our example.

Exercise:

Find this voicing for C7, F7, Bflat7, D7, and A7.

Notice that the notes for both voicings consist of the same notes, the only difference is that the 7th and sharpened 9th are at the bottom of the first voicing, and they are at the top of the second voicing.

Exercise

Now we have found out how to find all the chords for the minor 2 -5 -1, **find the following**, but use the second voicing you studied for the 7th sharp 9 & 5 chord (3, sharp 5, 7, sharp 9) because this will provide a smoother progression.

1. 2-5-1 in C minor = D minor 7 flat 5 – G7 sharp 9 & 5 – C minor 7.... To help you with this first task, this should be D minor 7 flat 5 = C, E, F, A flat; then G7 sharp 9 & 5 = B, D sharp, F, A sharp; then C minor 7 = B flat, D, E flat, G.

2. 2-5-1 in G minor = A minor 7 flat 5 – D7 sharp 9 & 5 – G minor 7.

3. 2-5-1 in F minor = G minor 7 flat 5 – C7 sharp 9 & 5 – F minor 7.

4. 2-5-1 in A minor = B minor 7 flat 5 – E7 sharp 9 & 5 – A minor 7.

There is a cheat method to find the middle chord (7th chord with sharp 5 and sharp 9 in 3,5,7,9 voicing). Here is the cheat method for C7 sharp 9 sharp 5. Left hand plays root of chord.

1. Right hand thumb on major 3rd of chord (E), while 5th finger reaches up one note less than an octave (E flat)

2. Middle notes relative to upper root (C) are down 2 steps (=a tone =B flat =the 7th of the chord) and then down 2 more steps (=a tone = G sharp = the sharpened 5th of the chord).

This gives us the RH chord, which is, from the bottom upwards, E, Gsharp, Bflat, Eflat. The left hand plays the root (low C).

Exercise:

Use this technique to find voicings for G7, F7, Bflat7, A7 and E7.

Although this cheat technique is quick and easy, it does little to help your grasp of how the notes relate to the root, so I would suggest you use it only when you have little time to find a lot of chords.

Autumn leaves progression

We have now learned all of the most essential jazz chords, and we can play a piece that uses both major and minor 2 – 5 – 1 progressions. Autumn leaves starts with a 2 -5 – 1 in B flat major, and then we have a minor 2 – 5 – 1 at the beginning of the second line. It will be useful to find the chords in their individual 2 – 5 – 1 sequences before we attempt the whole piece, so here is a useful strategy:

1. Find the 2 – 5 – 1 in B flat major, i.e. C minor 7 - F7 - B flat major 7. Remember that from the C minor chord, all you need to do is to move you thumb down one step to find the F7 chord. For the C minor chord you should have B flat, D, E flat and G; for the F7 chord you should have A, D, E flat and G; for the B flat major chord you should have A, C, D and F.

2. Find the E flat major chord in 3, 5, 7, 9 voicing. Remember that the 3 and 5 are found in the major triad, and the major 7th is down a single step from the upper root, and finally put the 9th on top (two steps above the upper E flat). This should give you G, B flat, D, F.

3. Find the 2 -5 – 1 in G minor. i.e. A minor 7 flat 5 – D7 sharp 5 & 9 – G minor 9. This was found in the last exercise we did, and for the A minor 7 flat 5 you should have G. B, C, E flat; for the D7 sharp 5 & 9 you should have F sharp, A sharp, C, F; for the G minor 7 chord you should have F, A, B flat and D.

4. At the end of the first line there is a G7 sharp 5 & 9. Follow the instructions for the first voicing for the 7th sharp 5 & 9 chord, (7, sharp 9, 3, sharp 5) this should give you F, A sharp, B, D sharp. This chord is preceded by a G minor chord, and notice how, as you change chords, the bottom note F stays in place, although everything else moves up a step. This is because the 5 becomes a sharp 5, the minor 3rd becomes a major 3rd, and the 9th becomes a sharpened 9th.

5. Finally, notice the 2 -5 patterns in the second line from the bottom , G minor 7 – C7 – F minor 7 – B flat 7. We covered these chords when we learned *Misty*, which you might like to refer to.

The complete Autumn Leaves progression

|C min7	|F7	|B flat maj7	|E flat maj7	
|A min7 flat 5	|D7 sharp5 & 9	|G min7	|G7 sharp 9 & 5	
|C min7	|F7	|B flat maj7	|E flat maj7	
|A min7 flat 5	|D7 sharp5 & 9	|G min7	|Gmin7	
|A min7 flat 5	|D7 sharp5 & 9	|G min7	|G7 sharp 9 & 5	
|C min7	|F7	|B flat maj7	|E flat maj7	
|A min7 flat 5	|D7 sharp5 & 9	|G min7 C7	|F min7 B flat7	
|E flat major 7	|A min7 flat5 – D7 sharp 9 & 5	G min7	|G min7*|

(* use G7 sharp 9 &5 if you are going back to the beginning of the sequence)

These chords can be played in the right hand while the left hand plays a 'rocking bass', (as in our version of Ladybird) to support it. For the C min7 bar the left hand might play four even notes, a low C, followed by the C an octave higher, the low C again, and then the higher C again. This bass and chord texture is ideal if you are asked to play in a duo context, where, for instance, a saxophone player could solo or play the tune over the top. You could play a piano solo by playing a G blues improvisation over the rocking bass, and this way you could provide a complete jazz performance.

1. Piano plays bass and chords while saxophone plays the tune.
2. Piano plays bass and chords while saxophone improvises.
3. Piano plays G blues solo over rocking bass figure. (Saxophone silent)
4. Piano plays bass and chords while saxophone plays the tune.

When you play your G blues solo over the rocking bass, you could also include a few chords in order to get more variety.

Lesson Sixteen:
The walking bass and the tritone substitution

Walking bass for Autumn Leaves

When we play jazz, rather than playing a rocking bass, we will play a walking bass. As beginners, it will be too challenging to play a solo over a walking bass, but you will probably be able to play chords over a walking bass, and this will provide a great texture for other players to solo over. The basic principle is to play the root of each chord (left hand) at the start of each bar, and to join these with three 'linking' notes. For example, a bass line for Autumn Leaves would have a C at the start of the first bar (C min7) then three linking notes to an F at the start of the second bar (F7) then three linking notes to a B flat at the start of the third bar (B flat maj7) etc.

Left hand bass line.

|C ? ? ? |F ? ? ? |B flat ? ? ? etc

To provide these linking notes, we can use two patterns, one which rises and another that falls. This way we can choose whether to walk up to the root above or walk down to the root below, and this will enable us to keep our walking bass within a suitable range, not too low or too high. When we are unable to use the linking pattern, for example the two G chords in bars 7 and 8, we will default to the rocking bass pattern.

Rising and falling patterns for walking bass

1. *Falling pattern.* We are playing Autumn leaves in B flat major/G minor, which uses the scale B flat, C, D, E flat, F, G, A, B flat. Notice the two flats, B flat and E flat. For our descending pattern we can simply walk down the scale. This will give us

|C B flat A G|F E flat D C| B flat A G F| E flat D C B flat| A... etc,

In theory we can play our walking bass for the first eight bars in this way, but in practice we would fall off the end of the piano.

2. *Rising pattern.* Here we can use a pattern 'tone, semitone, semitone', providing

|C D E flat E natural |F G A flat A natural| B flat C C sharp D|E flat F F sharp G| A B C C sharp| D E F F sharp| G G G G|G G G G | .

Notice that the pattern becomes a little irregular when we move from the E flat chord to the A chord, because the gap between the chord roots (E flat and A) is larger than a 4th. All the other patterns rise a perfect 4th. Also notice that we use our default rocking bass when there are two bars of G.

These patterns will help you to provide a strong bass line whenever you are confronted with similar chord progressions. The Autumn Leaves progression pattern is one of an almost unbroken cycle of 5^{ths,} - starting on C, down a 5th to F, down a 5th to B flat, down a 5th to E flat etc, and because of this it offers us an ideal exercise to start our walking bass practise. Practise the first 16 bars before reading on.

If you look at the Autumn leaves progression bottom line, and the penultimate line, you will notice several occasions where there are two chord changes per bar. Again, at the start of each chord we will play the root, but this time our linking note (only one) can be a single step above the new root.

So for

|Gmin7 C7 |Fmin7 Bflat7 | E flat major7|

We have a situation |G ? C ? |F ? B flat ?|E flat

we can play (in left hand)| G, D flat, C, G flat, |F, B, B flat, E, |E flat,

and for

|Amin7 flat 5 D7Sharp 5 and 9| G min7 |

we can play (in left hand)| A, E flat, D, A flat,| G.

The tritone substitution

This is a device which is mentioned frequently in jazz circles, often the discussion is accompanied by perplexed expressions from people who don't know what it is, and smug expressions from people who do. It really isn't complicated – let me explain.

1. For the chord of C7 we need a root, a 3rd, and a 7th. These are the only notes essential to the identity of the chord. Go to a piano and play the root (C) in your left hand, while your right hand plays the 3rd (E) and 7th (B flat).

2. Now, left hand, instead of playing C, play a G flat. Notice that this is now an identifiable G flat 7 chord, because the E is the 7th, and the B flat is the 3rd of the G Flat chord. The left hand is playing the root, G flat.

If you understand this, then you have just learned the principle of the tritone substitution. However, let's take things a little further:

(Tritone substitution continued)

To the chord of C7 we can add a 9th, the note D, giving us E, B flat and D (bottom upwards). If we change the left hand root to a G flat, the D will become a sharpened 5th relative to the G flat.

To this chord, E, B flat and D, we can add a 6th, (an A), giving us E, A, B flat and D. If we change the left hand root to a G flat, the A will become a sharpened 9th relative to the G flat.

Now we know this, we can see that a C7 chord voiced E, A, B flat, D in the right hand will become a G flat 7 chord with a sharpened 9th and 5th if the left hand plays a G flat, this Gflat chord is voiced 7, sharp 9, 3, sharp 5 voicing.

This means that **whenever we have a 7th chord, we can replace the root with another root a diminished 5th (= tritone) away while the right hand remains unchanged.**

Relating this to the 2 – 5 – 1 progression we can see that **D min7 – G7 – C maj7** can become **D min7 – D flat 7 - C major 7**, simply by playing a D flat in the left hand under the G7 chord instead of G. notice that the left hand is simply falling in semitone steps. So, in Autumn leaves we can experiment replacing 7th chords in this way. We can:

1. Replace F7 with B7. This means that C min – F7 – B flat maj will become C min – B7 – B flat maj. The right hand plays the same notes as before, but the left hand plays B instead of F.

2. Replace D7 with A flat 7, giving Amin7 flat5 – Aflat7 – Gmin.

3. Replace G7 with D flat 7, giving Dflat7 – Cmin.

4. Replace C7 with G flat 7 (penultimate line).

5. Replace B flat 7 with E7 (penultimate line). By replacing C7 with G flat 7 and B flat 7 with E7 the progression Gm –C7 –Fm – Bflat7 – Eflat Maj becomes Gmin – Gflat 7 – Fmin – E7 – E flat maj. Again the right hand plays the same as before. Notice that the left hand is descending smoothly, step by step in semitones.

Solo version of Autumn Leaves using shells

If we are performing alone, we can support our right hand by using shells in the left hand. The shells can be just roots at the bottom of the left hand with a 7th on top, the 7th being 2 steps below the upper root, with the exception of the major 7th chords where the 7th is only one step down below the upper root. For example, for the C min7 the left hand would play C and Bflat, for the F7 the left hand would play F and Eflat, then for the Bflat maj7 chord the left hand would play Bflat and A.

We can play each left hand shell at the start of each bar while the right hand improvises in G blues.

Lesson Seventeen:
11th chords

One particularly striking modern jazz sound is produced by the 11th chord. The 11th note of the chord is the same note as the fourth, as we will shortly see. You may have heard of the suspended fourth; this is where in a triad, the 3rd has been replaced by a 4th. For example, the C major triad (normally C, E, G) will become C, F, G. This is a very modern sound, because the 3rd, which normally identifies major/minor tonality, is not present. The 4th also has a strong desire to resolve to a 3rd, and because of this there is tension in the chord. The basic suspended chord (C, F, G) is often referred to as a sus chord. The 11th chord is a slightly extended version of this.

If we build up a C7 chord, and on top of this we add a 9th and an 11th, we will have the notes C, E, G, B flat, D, F, giving us 1, 3, 5, 7, 9, 11. This chord doesn't sound good because of the clash between the E and the F, so when we play this 11th chord we usually omit the 3rd, giving us C, G, B flat, D, F. This chord sounds good, and is the full version of C11. Notice that it might also be, and often is, described as a basic G minor 7 chord (G, B flat, D, F) over a C bass. Thus we can describe an 11th chord as a root with a minor 7 (1, 3, 5, 7) chord built up on the 5th of the chord.

Exercise

As C11 is Gmin7 over a C bass, we see that we can find an 11th chord by finding the root (C) and then finding the 5th of the chord (G) and then building up a minor 7th chord on this 5th (i.e. building up a Gmin7 chord 1, 3, 5, 7,). Using this technique, find a D11 chord, then an A11 chord, then an F11 chord

In addition to leaving out the 3rd, we can also leave out the 5th of the C11 chord, giving us C, B flat, D, F. This can also be described as a B flat major triad over a C bass.

Exercise

Notice that this last voicing of C11 is fairly simple to find: for this voicing of any 11 chord we can play the root in the left hand and build a major triad on the 7th. For example, finding G11, our left hand will play G and our right hand will play an F major triad. Now find this voicing for F11, A11, and D11.

To help you, for an F11 in this voicing, left hand would play a root, and right hand would play an E flat major triad (= a major triad on the 7th of the chord)

Soloing over an 11 chord, we will use a mixolydian mode (=major scale with flattened 7th) because the basic chord is still a 7th chord.

Free improvisation using 11th chords

Find a random selection of 11th chords, and notice how freely you can move from one 11th chord to any other 11th chord you choose. Because there is no 3rd in the chord, it has no strong 'gravitational pull'.

If your left hand is fairly large, you could re-voice the triad and play an 11th chord in your left hand alone. For example for C11, you will put C at the bottom, and then on top of this a B flat triad voiced F, B flat, D. So the complete chord will be C, F, B flat, D, from the bottom up. You could set up a latin, or a rock groove in your left hand, and your right hand can improvise in C mixolydian. This can be moved to any other key of your choice. Because both C11 and C9 are almost the same chord, the F in your left hand voicing here could move to E, giving a 4-3 resolution, then it might return to F. All this time, the right hand can improvise in C mixolydian.

Maiden Voyage by Herbie Hancock is a piece built almost entirely on 11th chords. A complete study of this is beyond the scope of this book, but I'll give you some hints on improvisation over the first two chords.

1. The first chord is a D11 chord. For this, left hand can play a D while the right hand plays an A minor 7 chord. For D11, we can play an A minor 1, 3, 5, 7 over our root D for the same reasons that we found we could play a G min 7 chord over a C to produce a C11 chord. We will go one step further and play this A min 7 in a 7, 9, 3, 5 voicing, giving the right hand G, B, C, E.

   The left hand can hop between playing the low D and the A minor chord in 7, 9, 3, 5, while the right hand improvises in D mixolydian , (D, E, F sharp, G, A, B, C, D).

2. The second chord is F11, for which the left hand can play F while the right hand can play a 7, 9, 3, 5 voicing for C minor 7 (B flat, D, E flat, G).

   As before, the left hand can hop between the root F and the C minor voicing, while the right hand improvises in F mixolydian, (F, G, A, B flat, C, D, E flat, F).

More about left hand voicings

When we improvise at the piano or keyboard, and assuming we have a bass player, our left hand can play chords such as 7, 9, 3, 5 voicings and 3, 5, 7, 9, voicings in the piano's mid-range, while our right hand improvises above it. We will want to keep our left hand in the piano's middle octave. The voicings for major and minor 2 – 5 – 1 that we have explored may sometimes take us outside this range. For example, if we were to find a 2 – 5 – 1 in E flat major, our chord 2, F minor, might feel either too high or too low if our right hand was improvising on top.

Another voicing for the 2 – 5 – 1 in a major key

Because of this, we sometimes start our major 2 – 5 – 1 with the chord 2 in a 3, 5, 7, 9 position. This time, instead of moving our thumb down, we move the second note from the top down a single step. This gives us a 7, 9, 3, 6 voicing for a chord 5. Here are some steps to clarify this. Left hand plays the roots while right hand plays the chords.

1. Find the chord 2 in 3, 5, 7, 9 position. For example, in C major you would find a D minor 7 chord voiced F, A, C, E,

2. Lower the second note from the top a single step (semitone) to give you a 7 chord voiced 7, 9, 3, 6. For example, in C major you would find a G7 chord voiced F, A, B, E.

3. Find your chord 1 in 3, 5, 7, 9 voicing. For example, in C major you would find a C major 7 chord voiced E, G, B, D.

Note that in a 3,5,7,9 voicing, the 3 and 5 (at the bottom of 3,5,7,9) are the top two notes of the basic triad (1,3,5) and the top two notes, 7 and 9, are 2 steps either side of the upper root, except for the final chord, a major 7th chord, (=chord one), where the 7th will be only a single step below the upper root.

Exercise

Find 2 – 5 – 1 progressions for F major, B flat major, E flat major, and G major using this set of voicings.

Exercise

Play the chords for Ladybird in the right hand, while left hand uses the rocking bass idea, but this time, when you play bars 3 and 4 (F minor 7 and B flat 7) use the new voicings for the 2 – 5 pattern. Similarly, use these new voicings for the D min 7 to G7 at the start of the last line.

Another voicing for a 2 – 5 – 1 in a minor key

1. Our chord 2 in the minor key is a minor 7th chord with a flattened 5th. To find a 3, 5, 7, 9 voicing for this, first find a 3, 5, 7, 9 voicing for the minor 7th chord, and then flatten the 5th. (The 5th is the second note from the bottom of the 3, 5, 7, 9 chord).

   For example, in C minor, our chord 2 is a D min 7 chord with a flattened 5th, which is voiced F. A flat, C, E.

2. Our chord 5 in the minor key is a chord of 7th chord type with a sharpened 5th and a sharpened 9th, and we will voice this 7, sharp 9, 3, sharp 5.

   For example, in C minor, our chord 5 is G7 with a sharpened 9th and 5th, voiced F, A sharp, B, D sharp. Tip: find major triad of the chord 5, replace the root with notes 2 steps each side (giving 7, 9, 3, 5) then sharpen 9 and 5.

3. Our chord 1 can be a regular minor 7 chord in a 3, 5, 7, 9 voicing.

   For example, in C minor we would play E flat, G, B flat, and D.

Exercise

Find a minor 2 – 5 – 1 for G minor, F minor, A minor, and D minor.

Exercise:

Apply these new voicings to Misty, Ladybird, and Autumn leaves

Concluding remarks

This tutor will serve to make it possible to understand the basics of improvisation, and I hope that I have managed to communicate my ideas clearly. My aim has been to offer you a completely new approach to playing the piano, and I sincerely hope that you will feel inspired to continue your journey into improvised music. The course I have provided in this book will offer you many ideas to explore, and will lay foundations which will enable you to learn advanced jazz modes and improvise completely freely at the piano.

Alternatively, you could use this knowledge as a basis for more classically oriented improvisation, and this might lead you into composing music of your own. Above all, you will have the freedom to do your own thing. Enjoy!

Appendix - additional help for more advanced players

The next section is a toolkit for aspiring jazz pianists, which also serves as an appendix of useful modes and introduces some more jazz chord voicings.

Tips on finding modes

This section is to help you after you have been playing for a few months. Having taught jazz piano to many students over years of teaching, I have discovered ways to make complicated modes less scary. I'll discuss the most common, beginning with basic modes and progressing to some advanced modes. Many other jazz courses choose to focus on the interval relationships between the notes of the scales, offering a sequence of tones and semitones for a student to memorise; whereas this is helpful, it does not help our ears to relate the notes of the scale to the root of the scale, so as an advance on this I have presented the modes as relating to various more easily identifiable frameworks. This will make it easier for the student to 'hear' to notes of the mode in relation to the root of the chord.

Ionian mode is the same as the major scale. This mode is used over a major 7th chord.

Mixolydian mode is a major scale with a flattened 7th. This mode is used over an un-altered 7th chord.

Dorian mode is the major scale with a flattened 3rd and flattened 7th. This mode is used over a minor 7th chord.

Aolian mode is the major scale with flattened 3rd, 6th, and 7th. This mode is used over a minor 7th chord.

Phrygian mode is the major scale with flattened 2nd, 3rd, 6th, and 7th. This can be used over a minor 7th chord in certain circumstances. It has a Spanish feel to it.

Locrian mode is the major scale with flattened 2nd, 3rd, 5th, 6th, 7th. This mode can be used over a minor 7th chord with a flattened 5th.

Lydian mode is the major scale with sharpened 4th. This can be used over a major 7th chord.

Exercise:

Choose one of these modes, and then find it starting on C, then starting on F, then starting on E flat, then starting on B flat. Work through all of these modes in this way, tackling one at a time.

Summary mode to chord application for basic chords

Over a **minor 7** chord, use either a dorian mode (major scale flat 3 and 7) or an aolian mode (major scale flat 3, 6, and 7 or a Phrygian mode (major scale flat 2, 3, 6 and 7) as appropriate.

Over a straight 7th chord, use a mixolydian mode (major scale flat 7).

Over a **major 7th** chord, use either a major scale or a lydian mode (major scale sharp 4) as appropriate.

The super locrian mode – used over 7th chord with altered 5th AND altered 9th

Over the 7th chord with a sharpened 5th and 9th we play the super locrian scale. This is sometimes called the altered scale or the diminished whole tone scale, and the very name, whichever one is chosen, terrifies many people. Let's lift the mystique.

1. Note 9 can be considered the same as the note 2. In the chord of C7 this would be a D.

2. Any 7th chord needs a root, a 3rd, and a 7th, so these notes will be included in the scale, forming a framework. For example, a C7 would require C, E, and B flat.

3. To the notes in this framework (C, E, and B flat) we add flat 2 and sharp 2, and flat 5 and sharp 5, For C7 this would mean adding D flat and D sharp, and also G flat and G sharp.

1 flat 2, sharp 2, **3**, flat 5, sharp 5, **7, 1**

C D flat, D sharp, **E**, G flat, G sharp, **B flat, C**

Exercise:

Find the super locrian modes for G7, F7, D7, and B flat 7,

The locrian sharp 2 mode - used over minor 7th chord with flattened 5th

Over the min7 flat 5 chord we use a locrian sharp 2 mode. We already know that the locrian mode is mode 7 of the major scale (using exclusively the white notes of C major scale, we found out that running from B to B we have B locrian), so to produce a locrian sharp 2 we have to find the locrian mode and then sharpen the 2nd degree. This is actually very difficult, so here is a short cut. I'm choosing the chord of A min7 flat 5 to use in order to demonstrate the principle. Remember that the melodic minor ascending scale is the same as the major scale with flattened 3rd.

1. Faced with the chord of A min7 flat 5, we need to find an A locrian scale with a raised 2nd degree.

2. Build a melodic minor ascending scale on the 3rd of the A min7 flat 5 chord.

    The 3rd of the chord is the note C, so we will find a C melodic minor ascending scale (=C major scale with flattened 3rd). This is C, D, E flat, F, G, A, B, C.

3. Run this scale from A to A. This will give us an A locrian sharp 2 mode, which is A, B, C, D, E flat, F, G, A.

We can test this, because we know it will be mode 7 of B flat major scale, with a raised 2nd degree.

Because we will always play the 3rd of the chord, from which we can find the melodic minor, you will find my shortcut a lot easier than finding relevant major scales and raising 2nd degrees.

Exercise:

Find locrian sharp 2 modes to fit over B min7 flat5, E min7 flat5, and Fsharp min7flat5.

The locrian sharp 2 and super locrian modes can be applied to chords 2 and 5 in a minor 2-5-1 respectively. Here is a summary to clarify this.

Summary of chords and modes for minor 2-5-1

1. Chord 2. Minor7 flat5. Use locrian sharp 2 mode.

2. Chord 5. 7th sharp 9 and sharp 5. Use super locrian mode.

3. Chord 1. Minor 7. Use Dorian mode.

The Lydian dominant mode – used over the 7th chord with sharpened 4th (= sharpened 11th)

Another common mode is the Lydian dominant mode, which is used over a 7th chord with a sharpened 11th, such as a C7 sharp 11. This is a major scale with a raised 4th and a flattened 7th, but let's see why this is:

1. An 11th is the same as a 4th. Because we are working over a 7th chord with a sharpened 11th (= sharp 4), the 4 is sharpened. This gives us an F sharp in the case of C7.

2. A 7th chord has a 7th which is down two steps from the root. This gives us a B flat in the case of C7.

3. Knowing this, we know that we need to find the major scale of the chord root, then sharpen the 4th and flatten the 7th. In the case of C7 sharp 11 we will find C major scale, and then sharpen the 4th and flatten the 7th, which gives us C, D, E, F sharp, G, A, B flat, C. This is the Lydian dominant scale.

Exercise:

Find Lydian dominant modes for F, G, D, and Bflat.

After these descriptions of super locrian, locrian sharp 2, and Lydian dominant modes, I will point out that all three of these modes are actually different modes of the melodic minor ascending scale. *Mode 4 of a melodic minor scale is a Lydian dominant, mode 6 is a locrian sharp 2, mode 7 is a super locrian.*

For example, taking C melodic minor scale, C, D, E flat, F, G, A, B, C:

If we find mode 4, - F, G, A, B, C, D, E flat, F, - we have an F Lydian dominant scale;

If we find mode 6, - A, B, C, D, E flat, F, G, A, - we have an A locrian sharp 2 mode:

If we find mode 7, - B, C, D, E flat, F, G, A, B, - we have a B super locrian mode

The Lydian augmented mode – used over the major 7th chord with sharpened 5th.

Another less commonly used mode of the melodic minor mode is mode 3, which gives us the Lydian augmented mode. For example, mode 3 of C melodic minor would be E flat Lydian augmented – E flat, F, G, A, B, C, D, E flat. This scale is used over a major 7th chord with a sharpened 5th. If we compare the Lydian augmented scale to the major scale (E flat major in our example) we find we have a major scale with a sharpened 4th and 5th. Let's see how we might apply this scale.

Given the chord of C major 7 sharp 5, (an octave below middle C, left hand play C, E, G sharp, B) we could improvise in the right hand using a C major scale with a sharpened 4th and 5th – C, D, E, F sharp, G sharp, A, B, C.

Exercise:

Find the Lydian augmented modes for F, D, G, and E flat.

The whole tone scale – used over 7th chord with altered 5th

When we have a 7th chord with an altered, i.e. flattened or sharpened 5th (and only an altered 5th) we can improvise using a whole tone scale. A whole tone scale is a scale where the intervals between the notes are all consecutive whole tones. E.g. a whole tone scale starting on C would be C, D, E, F sharp, G sharp, A sharp, C.

Notice that the C7 chord with a 9th, and flattened and sharpened 5th, actually IS a whole tone scale if the 9th is taken down an octave!

Exercise:

Find whole tone scales starting on F, D, and Eflat.

The diminished scale – used over the diminished chord and the 7th flat 9 chord

The diminished 7th chord is a stack of minor 3rds. For example, a C diminished chord would be C, E flat, G flat, A.

The diminished scale is built using the notes of the chord as a frame. To this frame, we add notes a tone (two steps) above each note of the diminished chord. So a C diminished scale would be **C**, D, **E flat**, F, **F sharp**, G sharp, **A**, B, **C**, the notes of the chord are in bold. This is sometimes called the whole/half diminished scale because of the semitone/tone recursive pattern.

Exercise:

Find the diminished scale starting on F, G, and A. Compare A diminished scale with C diminished scale. What do you notice?

If we have a **7th chord with a flattened 9th**, for example C7 flat 9 (=C, E, G, B flat, D flat) we notice that we have an E diminished chord over a C. Because of this, we can use an E diminished scale when we improvise over this chord. **E**, F sharp. **G**, A, **B flat**, C, **D flat**, E flat, E. Again, I have written the notes of E diminished chord in bold. In spite of this relationship, it is of course easier if we find a mode which starts on C, i.e. the root of the chord.

So, if we are confronted with a 7th chord with a flattened 9th, for example C7 flat 9 (=C, E, G, B flat, D flat) we can see that it would be easier to find a scale that started on C. Now then, If we run the E diminished scale from C to C we get the notes C, D flat, D sharp, E, F sharp, G, A, B flat and C. The top four notes of this scale are the same as C mixolydian, the bottom five are the same as C super locrian.

Another way to find this scale is to find the C diminished chord (C, E flat, F sharp, A, C) and to add notes a semitone above each note of the chord. (=**C**, D flat, **E flat**, E, **F sharp**, G , **A** , B flat, **C**) again the notes of the C diminished chord are in bold. Because of this, this scale is sometimes called the half/whole diminished.

Exercise:

Find this scale starting on F, G, and Eflat.

You will see that the whole/half and the half/whole diminished scales are in fact the same scale beginning at different points. Contrary to what you might hear, these are not two different scales(they are the same) and they are not interchangeable.

Notice that if we have a C7 chord with only an altered 5th, we will use a whole tone scale; if we have a C7 chord with only an altered 9th, we will use a diminished scale; if we have a C7 chord with **both 5th and 9th altered**, we will use a super locrian scale, which is actually a mixture of the two - the first half of the scale is diminished to accommodate the altered 9th (=flattened and sharpened 2nd) and the upper portion of the scale is whole tone to accommodate the altered 5th.

The 5th mode of the harmonic minor scale – used over the 7th flat 9 chord

Over a 7th chord with a flattened 9th (e.g. C7 flat9 = C, E, G, B flat, D flat) we have another scale option - the 5th mode of the harmonic minor. In the case of C7 flat 9 this is mode 5 of F harmonic minor, which is C, D flat, E, F, G, A flat, B flat, C (i.e. F harmonic minor starting and finishing on its 5th note, which is a 'C'). We can see that if we compare this mode to a C major scale, we have a flattened 2nd, 6th, and 7th. This mode has a curious eastern feel, and is very useful for pieces such as Caravan by Duke Ellington. We dabbled with a similar set of sounds when we played the second piece (lesson two) in this book.

Additional jazz voicings, available when a bass player is present.

When playing jazz chords, the easiest way to find effective voicings is to leave the roots for the bass player to play, this means that our left hand can play the 3rds and 7ths of the chords and our right hand can build up an effective jazz extension.

Given that the left hand is playing the 3rd and 7th, there are two ways in which the right hand can extend the chords:

1. Using a stack of 4ths. E.g. if the left hand is playing a C7 chord (E and B flat, giving 3rd and 7th) the right hand could build up a stack of 4ths from a D, playing D, G, and C, from the bottom upwards.

2. Using a triad in root position or a triad in an inversion. For example, if we are playing a C altered chord (C7 with sharpened 5th and sharpened 9th), the left hand can play the basic C7 chord (E and B flat, giving 3rd and 7th) and the right hand can play a major triad based on the sharpened 5th (= G sharp = A flat) i.e. an A flat major triad.

We will look at the most frequently used chords and see how we might extend these, given that in each case the bass player will play the root, our left hand will play the 3rd and 7th, and our right hand will play the extension.

7th chords

For simple 7th chords, our right hand can play a stack of 4ths built on either the 2nd, the 3rd, or the 6th. For example, when playing a C7 chord, the left hand will play the 3rd and 7th, (E and B flat) or a 7,9,3,6 or 3,6,7,9 voicing, and the right hand can play a stack of 4ths built on either:

1. The 2nd (for C7, the 2nd=D, so a stack of 4ths would give us D, G, C, from the bottom up).

2. The 3rd (for C7, the 3rd=E, so a stack of 4ths would give us E, A, D, from the bottom up).

3. The 6th (for C7, the 6th=A, so a stack of 4ths would give us A, D, G from the bottom up).

Exercise: Find a G7 chord, left hand playing 3rd and 7th (B and F), or a 7,9,3,6 (F,A,B,E) or 3,6,7,9 (B,E,F,A) voicing, and then find three different stacks of 4ths in your right hand. You should have A, D, G, and B, E, A and E, A, D.

Alternatively, in order to extend a 7th chord we can play the minor triad based on the 5th. For example, over a C7 chord we could play a G minor triad in any inversion we choose. So given C7, the right hand could play G, B flat, D, or B flat, D, G, or D, G, B flat. All chords are presented from the bottom upwards.

Exercise

Given a G7 chord, left hand plays B and F, find the right hand voicings for the minor triad based on the 5th. You should find D, F, A, and F, A, D, and A, D, F. Now do the same for C7 and F7.

For altered 7th chords (5th and 9th are sharpened/flattened) we can build a stack of 4ths on the 7th, or the sharpened 9th, or the sharpened 5th. So, as an example, for C7 sharp 9 our right hand could play:

1. A stack of 4ths built on the 7th. For C7 this would be B flat, and E flat, and A flat.

2. A stack of 4ths built on the sharpened 9th. For C7 this would be E flat, and A flat, and D flat.

3. A stack of 4ths built on the sharpened 5th. For C7 this would be A flat, and D flat and G flat.

All right hand chords are presented from the bottom note upwards. Again, the left hand will play the 3rd and 7th, or one of the two voicings for 7 chords with sharpened 9 &5 discussed in the section about the minor 2 – 5 – 1.

Exercise:

Find three stacks of 4ths for an altered G7 chord, i.e., find stacks of 4ths built on the 7th, the sharpened 9th, and the sharpened 5th. The left hand will play the 3rd and 7th = B and F. You should find F, B flat, and E flat, and B flat, E flat, and A flat, and E flat, A flat, and D flat. Then do the same for C7.

Alternatively, we can extend the altered 7th chord by building minor triads on the flattened 9th or the sharpened 9th, or we can build major triads on the flattened 5th or the sharpened 5th. Of these four options, the most commonly used is the major triad on the sharpened 5th. For example, given a chord of C7, the left hand will play the 3rd and 7th (E and B flat) while the right hand can play an A flat major triad in any inversion (A flat, C, E flat, or C, E flat, A flat, or E flat, A flat, C).

Exercise:

Given the chord of an altered G7, the left hand will play B and F, or appropriate 7,9,3,5/3,5,7,9 with sharp9&5; in you right hand, find inversions for the major triad based on the 5th. This should be a triad of E flat and the notes should be E flat, G B flat, or G, B flat, E flat, or B flat, E flat and G.

7th chord with flattened 9th

For this chord we can find a major triad built on the 6th, normally in an inversion which has the 3rd of the triad at the top. For example, over a C7 flat 9 chord we might have an A major triad with C sharp at the top, i.e., right hand from the bottom up we will have E, A, C sharp, the left hand playing the 3rd and 7th (E and B flat). The left hand will play 3rd and 7th, and possibly also root and 5th if required.

For minor 7th chords, one option would be to play the 'so what' chords described earlier. Alternatively, while left hand plays the 3rd and 7th, right hand can build a stack of 4ths on the root, or the 2nd, or the 4th, or the 5th. Also we can build patterns of 4ths belonging to a mode, like we did when we played 'Mixolydian Funk'.

The minor 7 chord and the minor 7th chord with the flattened 5th can both be extended with a major triad based on the 7th. So over a C minor 7 chord, or a C minor 7 flat 5 chord, we could play a B flat major triad in any inversion. Similarly, over a D minor 7 chord or D minor 7 flat 5 chord we might play a C major triad.

Exercise:

Extend Dmin7 in this way, and then do the same for Fmin7 and G min7.

The minor 7 chord can also be extended by building another minor 7 chord based on the 2nd on top of the minor 7 chord; so for a C minor 7 chord the left hand could play 3rd and 7th (E flat and B flat) or a 7,9,3,5 (Bflat, D, Eflat, G) or a 3,5,7,9 (Eflat, G, Bflat, D) while the right hand plays a D minor 7 chord on top of this (=D, F, A, C). Left hand could alternatively play a basic 1,3,5,7 voicing (C, Eflat, G, Bflat).

Over the minor 7 chord with a flattened 5th we can play a minor flat 5 triad based on the 2nd; for example, over C minor 7 flat 5 (left hand 3rd and 7th = E flat and B flat, or possibly 1,3,5,7 =C, Eflat, Gflat, Bflat) right hand would play a D minor flat 5 triad (= D, F, A flat).

Exercise:

Extend Fmin7 flat5 in this way, then do the same for Dmin7 flat5.

Another particularly nice voicing for the minor 7th chord is based on stacks of 5ths. Here, the left hand will play a stack of 5ths based on the root and the right hand will play a stack of 5ths based on the minor 3rd; for example, for a voicing of C minor 7, the left hand will play C, G, D and the right hand will play E flat, B flat, and F.

Exercise:

Using this last voicing, find a voicing for D minor 7. You should find that your left hand plays D, A, E, and your right hand plays F, C, G.

Yet another great voicing for the min7 chord is found by finding the 7, 9, 3, 5 or 3, 5, 7, 9 voicings (see p26) and then replacing the 5th with a 4th. This leaves 7, 9, 3, 4 (e.g. Bflat, D, Eflat, F for C min7) or 3, 4, 7, 9 (e.g. Eflat, F, Bflat, D for C min7). Inversions of this chord are also very effective.

Exercise:

Find these voicings for D min7 and A min7. For D min7 you should have C, E, F, G and then F, G, C, E, and then for A min7 you should have G, B, C, D and then C, D, G, B.

Over major 7th chords our right hand can play stacks of 4ths based on the 2nd, or the 3rd, or the 6th. Alternatively, we can play the major triad of the 5th in any inversion. For example, in playing a C major 7 chord, the left hand will play the 3rd and 7th, (E and B) or 7,9,3,5/3,5,7,9, and the right hand will play an inversion of a G major triad. In many contexts we can also use the major triad of the 2nd in any inversion – this has Lydian implications, and will work in most cases, unless the major 7th chord is serving as a key chord. For example, for an F major 7 chord, our left hand can play the 3rd and 7th (A and E) while the right hand plays a G major triad, G, B, D, or B, D, G, or D, G, B. This is a particularly pleasant chord, and you might like to go back to the film music improvisation and experiment by playing G major triad inversions in your right hand while your left hand plays the accompaniment riff in F. This will enable you to gain a feel for the nature of this wonderful harmonic effect.

The 7th chord with sharpened 11th (sometimes called a 7th with sharpened 4th)

Whenever we have a sharpened 11th (= sharp 4th) in a chord or scale, there is an implication of a major triad based on the 9th (= 2nd). For example, over a C7 sharp 11 chord we could play a D major triad (any inversion), and similarly over a C major 7 sharp 11 chord we could play a D major triad. The modes used to improvise over these would similarly include the raised 4th. For example, over a C major chord with a sharp 11 we would use the major scale with a sharpened 4th (the Lydian mode), and over a C7 sharp 11 chord we would use a major scale with a sharpened 4th and flattened 7th (the Lydian dominant mode). A good piece to use in order to study this chord is The Girl From Ipanema.

Additional substitutions similar to the tritone substitution

Earlier in the book, we discovered that if we had a C7 chord, we could change it into a G flat 7 chord simply by playing a bass G flat instead of the C root. We have also just discovered how we can extract a range of modes from a melodic minor scale. These links extend to the associated chords too. If we take a chord of B7, with a sharpened 5th and 9th, the right hand will play 3, sharp5, 7, and sharp 9, giving us D sharp, G, A, D, while the left hand provides the root B. If we were to improvise over this we could use a B super locrian mode. Keeping the right hand chord in place, we can alter the root to produce different chord sounds.

1. If the left hand plays a C root, the right hand notes will be interpreted as a C minor chord voiced 3, 5, 6, 9. Over this we would play on a C melodic minor ascending scale.

2. If the left hand plays an F root, the right hand notes would be interpreted as an F7 chord voiced 7, 9, 3, 13. Over this we would play on an F Lydian dominant scale.

3. If the left hand plays an E flat root, the right hand notes would be interpreted as an E flat major chord voiced 1, 3, flat 5, maj7, over which we could play an E flat Lydian augmented, or an ordinary Lydian mode.

Notice how we can keep the harmony and the scales the same (C melodic minor ascending in this case), while we alter the bass notes to produce new chords and new sounds.

Putting it all together

Having been introduced to many chords and many modes, we need to practise applying our knowledge so that we can find them without having to consciously work them out every time. The skills you have developed through working out the chords and modes will have considerably developed your grasp of 'keyboard geography', and it is now time to practise using these chords and modes so that your fingers will find the notes automatically. Here are a few ideas to help you achieve this.

Practise the 2-5-1 sequences, major and minor versions, in both voicings. Play the chords in the left hand while the right hand plays the appropriate mode on top. i.e.

1. Major 2-5-1. **Chord 2** is a minor 7 chord, right hand will use dorian mode. **Chord 5** is a 7th chord, right hand will use mixolydian mode. **Chord 1** is a major 7th, right hand will play notes from the major scale.

2. Minor 2-5-1. **Chord 2** is a minor7 chord with a flattened 5th, right hand will use a locrian sharp 2 mode. **Chord 5** is a 7th chord with sharp 5 and sharp 9, right hand will use a super locrian mode. **Chord 1** is a minor 7th chord, right hand will use a dorian mode.

   For the chord 1 in a minor 2-5-1 we might alternatively choose a minor 6 chord (=minor triad with a 6th added) or a minor chord with a major 7th. In these cases we would use a melodic minor ascending mode (=major scale with flattened 3rd). Also experiment playing a major 2-5 moving to a min chord 1, and a minor 2-5 moving to a major chord 1.

   This practise is best if you have a bass line, which you might be able to record into your keyboard. Alternatively you could buy one of Jamey Aebersold's CDs from a music shop – this will provide you with a recorded bass line played by one of the leading musicians in New York City.

Any 7th chord can be almost freely replaced by any other type of 7th chord. For example, in the middle of the major 2-5-1 you could play a 7 sharp 5 sharp 9 (= altered chord), or you could play your regular chord with a flattened 9th. Select right hand modes from those discussed in the 'tips on finding modes' section.

   You could play Autumn leaves, chords in the left hand, right hand trying out various appropriate modes as you experiment. Mr Aebersold's CDs can provide the bass line. You could replace the F7 with a 7 sharp 9 sharp 5 chord and use F super locrian over the top.

   In fact, you will now be ready to tackle all of the Aebersold CDs, enabling you to learn all of the standard jazz tunes.

About ear training

To develop the highest level of improvisational skill we need to be able to hear notes and melodic lines in our heads, and many jazz courses will emphasise this at the expense of working on other important skills. There are a number of ear training courses for jazz musicians, and I would suggest that an aspiring jazz musician invest in several, but before you rush out to buy these, I have something important to say!

Remember the comment I made earlier about the drummers that I taught, and how these players progressed faster than the classical musicians? – One of these classical musicians was a fantastic violinist, possessing an incredible sense of pitch, and if I whistled a tune they could have played it back to me immediately and flawlessly. The fact that these talented musicians had such difficulty improvising was an important lesson for me. I subsequently learned that the most helpful teaching technique for students wanting to improvise well was (drum roll please) to make them sit down and improvise. This is the approach I have adopted in this book.

This having been said, let's talk about ear training. We can approach this from several angles. Conventionally this has been divided into three sections:

1. Work on rhythm. This involves copying, and ultimately writing down the rhythm of a piece of music.

2. Work on harmony. Starting with the bass line, we can build up to writing down the harmonic sequence of a piece of music.

3. Work on melody. We sing back, and ultimately write down the melodic line that we hear.

Taking this as a starting point, we can develop a more sophisticated system for developing the skills required for jazz:

1. We can sing a scale and work around the notes in this scale, keeping the root in our minds as a reference point. For example, using the major scale, we can label the notes in ascending order as 1,2,3,4,5,6,7,8, and we could then set ourselves a sequence of notes to sing. For example, if I set you the task of singing notes of degrees 1,1,5,5,6,6,5,4,4,3,3,2,2,1, you should find yourself singing twinkle twinkle little star.

Exercise

Sing these degrees of the major scale in order: 1,2,3,1,1,2,3,1,3,4,5,3,4,5,5,6,5,4,3,1,5,6,5,4,3,1

We can use this concept to help us to become familiar with all of the difficult modes, working at each mode in turn, and setting ourselves the task of singing various sets of notes from that mode.

We can develop this idea even further to build the skills we need for more complicated modes. Whereas in the simple scales we might only use the root as a reference point, when faced with, for example, a super locrian scale, we could use the root as a primary reference point, but also we could use the 3rd and the 7th as secondary reference points. Having built this frame of 1, 3, 7 in our minds, we can pin the flattened and sharpened 2nd and flattened and sharpened 5th to this. This technique will not only make it easier to pitch the notes of this scale, but also increase the accuracy of our pitch. Similarly, if we are working on the diminished scale, we could use a diminished chord for a set of reference points.

2. We can listen to various songs, and see if we can identify the roots of the chords. As we become more advanced, we will be able to identify the 2 – 5 – 1 progressions as they occur, then we will learn various other harmonic patterns, and then ultimately we will be able to work out a chord sequence simply by listening to a tune a few times

3. We can work on identifying melodic intervals without reference to any scale or chord, working on being able to sing a string of notes set at random intervals apart, referring only to the previous note and pitching the next note from this alone. For example we could sing a C, then move up a major 3rd to an E, then move down a 5th to an A, the move up a diminished 5th to an E flat, and then move up a minor 7th to a D flat etc.

4. Having worked on all three of these, we can start to sing melodic lines over bass lines. We could programme a bass line into our keyboard, and then play it back for us to sing over.

5. We can listen to famous jazz solos, listening first to the melodic lines, and then to the harmony (or vice versa), and then we can work out how to reproduce these sounds on the piano.

6. We can listen to famous jazz solos, listening first to the melodic lines, and then to the harmony (or vice versa), and then we can write them down, using the piano to help us to find the notes.

7. We can listen to famous jazz solos, listening first to the melodic lines, and then to the harmony (or vice versa), and then we can write down these sounds without reference to any instrument. I will allow you to use a tuning fork!

8. We can learn jazz solos by repetitive listening alone, and having heard a solo a few times we will be able to go to the piano and play it from memory. This skill usually takes a considerable amount of work to acquire.

Above all, the most important thing is to listen to a lot of music, since it is only through listening that we can programme our minds to recognise the various sounds that we are working with. Also, transpose things you play into different keys.

I hope that I have made your musical journey a lot easier than mine, and I hope that this book will inspire you to produce some exciting improvisations.

A little bit more

This book is the product of years of teaching, and many sections were revised over the year that this was in private use before publication. Although the book is now in the process of being published there are several ideas that I would have liked to have developed further, but having seen the book grow to over 30,000 words I don't think I'll add much more. I'll outline several ideas I would like to have discussed further.

- When discussing the middle chord of the minor 2-5-1, referred to as 'the altered chord', I only discussed the 7th chord with raised 5th and 9th. Now then, we could just as easily have flattened the 5th and 9th, or maybe raised one and flattened the other. It is called 'the altered chord' simply because both the 5th and 9th are altered.

For example, we can find a basic 7th chord by finding the major triad (1,3,5) and then replacing the bottom note (root) with notes two steps each side(to replace the root with 7 and 9 - e.g. C7 would be Bflat, D, E, and G voiced 7,9,3,5 from bottom upwards). From this chord we can sharpen the 9th (D) and 5th (G), or flatten them both, or sharpen one and flatten the other. This would give us a 7,9,3,5 voicing of an altered chord.

Similarly we could find a 3,5,7,9 voicing by finding the major triad, taking the root up an octave, then replacing this upper root with notes two steps each side to find 7 and 9 (e.g. C7 in 3,5,7,9 voicing would be E,G, Bflat and D), and from here we can alter the 5th (G) and 9th (D).

Of course there are some chords where only the 5th or only the 9th will be altered.

- In the book I draw connections between mode names and various chords, e.g. for a minor 7th chord I suggest a dorian mode. This is correct, BUT, rather than knowing the name of the mode, it is actually more useful to know how the mode differs from the major scale and how it has been adjusted to fit the chord. For example a minor 7th chord has a minor 3rd and a 7th which is two steps below the upper root, so in order to find a mode which fits we have to adjust the major scale's 3rd to a minor 3rd and lower its 7th another step .

With this in mind, when asking students to find a mode I set them the task of finding a mode to fit the chord BEFORE getting them to name it. This is because if they have to name the correct mode to fit a chord we introduce an unnecessary step which makes the connection between chord and mode less obvious. It is better to see how a mode grows out of a chord than to have a head full of uncertain names of modes which might fit!

- When we have a long stretch of a single chord, we can tweak the notes in the chord to increase the variety in sounds available to us – provided that the 3rd and 7th stay in place. For example, a C7 chord with a mixolydian mode on top could move to a C7 chord with a flattened or sharpened 5th with a whole-tone scale on top, then it could move back to C7 with mixolydian. Alternatively we could have moved to a C7 flat9 chord and played a diminished scale, or we could have moved to a C7 altered chord (altered 5 th AND 9th) and played a super locrian mode. Also we can move from any of these chords to any other at any time, all we need to do is to make sure that the right hand notes agree with the left hand notes. If the left hand chord only has the 3rd and 7th, the right hand can freely move from mode to mode - because the left hand doesn't contain 5ths or 9ths which are the notes we are tweaking. If the bass is only a single note, forming a 'pedal point', (no other notes supporting the right hand) the right hand is free to play almost anything!

- Similarly, if the left hand is playing a minor 7 chord while the right hand plays dorian, the lefthand might move the 7th up a step to a major 7th, and the right hand will move to a mode with a major 7th in (but min 3rd) like for example the melodic minor ascending mode. After a bar or so in this mode we can move back to the ordinary minor 7th chord with dorian on top.

- Also, in a long stretch of a major 7th chord we might temporarily raise the 5th while the right hand moves to a Lydian augmented chord.